Type 2 Diabetes Cookbook for Beginners

1800 of Days Quick, Easy and Tasty Diabetes Recipes that Anyone can Cook at Home with a 28-Day Meal Plan included for Beginners and Advanced Users

Rosalinda Sherman

Table of Contents

INTRODUCTION

A diabetes diagnosis can undoubtedly be scary, especially when first diagnosed. Over the years, I've found that much fear comes from the unknown and stories of complications caused by long periods of uncontrolled blood sugar. People with unchecked diabetes risk heart disease, stroke, vision loss, depression, kidney failure, and other problems.

One research showed that it was much more likely for students who missed breakfast or had an erratic eating routine involving skipping meals daily to feel exhaustion. It's also crucial that you eat enough food during the day to sustain yourself. The lack of calories and vital nutrients, such as iron, will result in severe dietary limitations, adversely affecting energy levels. A diet based on whole grains helps your health and energy balance with nutritious foods. A diet rich in refined foods will adversely influence energy levels.

What are the many forms of diabetes? One of the most often asked topics on Diabetic South Africans is the many forms of diabetes. Type-2 Diabetes is a common illness that inhibits your body's capacity to utilize insulin properly. Patients with Type-2 Diabetes are characterized as having insulin resistance. People in their 40s and 50s are more likely to get this kind of diabetes. Earlier, it was referred to as adult-onset diabetes. On the other hand, Type-2 Diabetes mostly impacts children and adolescents owing to childhood obesity.

When your body either does not produce enough insulin or does not utilise it as it should, diabetes can develop. Chronic medical disease called diabetes impacts how your body converts food into energy.

Type 1, type 2, and gestational diabetes are the different types of diabetes (diabetes while pregnant).

Diabetes Type 1

Your body wrongly attacks itself, which results in Type-1 Diabetes, which stops your body from making insulin. About 5 to 10 percent of patients with diabetes have type 1 diabetes. The signs of type 1 diabetes might arise suddenly. The most often impacted age groups are kids, teenagers, and young adults. You need to take medicines every day to stay alive if you have Type 1 diabetes. Sadly, no one currently understands how to prevent Type 1 diabetes.

Diabetes Type 2

When you have Type-2 Diabetes, your body cannot effectively use insulin to keep your blood sugar levels within a reasonable range. 90% to 95% of patients with diabetes have type 2 diabetes. It develops over a number of years, and an adult is diagnosed with it. It is essential to check your blood sugar if you are at risk since you might not detect any symptoms. Making healthy lifestyle changes, such as losing weight, eating nutrient-dense meals, and exercising regularly, can prevent or delay the onset of Type-2 Diabetes.

Gestational Diabetes

Gestational diabetes properly develops in pregnant women who have never had diabetes. However, your kid may be more prone to health issues if you have gestational diabetes. Gestational Diabetes typically resolves after your baby is delivered, but it raises your chance of developing Type-2 diabetes later in life. In addition, your child is more likely to be obese as a child or adolescent and more likely to acquire Type-2 Diabetes later in life.

Your chances of obesity, diabetes, and heart disease may also be raised by consuming high quantities of added sugar, so reducing added sugar in your diet benefits your energy levels and your health. Try eliminating foods rich in added sugar to keep the energy levels more stable and decrease fatigue. Although the exact cause of type 2 diabetes is still not fully understood, being obese and overweight is believed to account for 80% of the risk of developing diabetes. So, if you have excess weight around your tummy, you are at greater risk of developing type 2 diabetes. In obese people, the abdominal fat cells have more nutrients than average, and this stress in the cell makes them release pro-inflammatory chemicals. These chemicals disrupt the function of the insulin hormone or make the body less sensitive to insulin. It is called insulin resistance, the primary cause of type 2 diabetes.
The diabetes nutrition and lifestyle education strategies you are about to learn will equip you with the tools you need to gain and maintain healthier habits for the rest of your life. Yes, you can change! You deserve the energy, confidence, and longevity that good health provides. Taking charge of your diabetes will yield immediate results that will continue to propel you forward as you make this a sustainable and enjoyable lifestyle.
Prevention is always better than cure. If you can stop developing diabetes before you have it, you will save yourself from a lifetime of being a prisoner to your body. It isn't even all that difficult.

Research has proven that if you are pre-diabetic, you can decrease the chances of the onset of type 2 diabetes by losing 7% of your body mass and following a moderate exercise routine. Something as easy as a daily walk around your neighborhood could save your life.

This is not a death sentence if you already have type 2 diabetes. You are not a "dead man walking," and by maintaining a healthy weight, engaging in regular exercise, and eating wisely, you can improve your body's acceptance of insulin, thereby decreasing the sugar levels in your blood. You can lock the moody diabetes teenager away and live a healthy and fulfilling life.

Treating diabetes is not about getting rid of some boogie in your life. Instead, it is about management.

Once diagnosed as diabetic, most people don't get magically diabetic. This means you can't hide in your closet and refuse to deal with the reality and impact of diabetes on your health.

You need to use medical treatment, dietary treatment, and a combination of physical activity and balanced mental health to maintain good health.

Imagine that you or your child has diabetes. In case you notice any diabetes signs, see your doctor. The sooner therapy can start, the sooner a problem can be discovered.

if you have previously received a diagnosis of diabetes.

As soon as you receive your diagnosis, you will need ongoing medical monitoring until your blood sugar levels return to normal.

You must first grasp how the body normally metabolizes glucose in order to understand diabetes.

People who with diabetes require medical guidance on how to treat their illness. Diabetes sufferers can manage their blood glucose levels by taking medicine, monitoring their diets, and engaging in physical activity.

Try Making Healthy Versions of Your Favorite Foods

You might feel like giving up on the foods you love because they're not healthy for you anymore. But why stop eating them altogether? Instead, try adding fruit to make healthier versions of your favorite foods. Just remember that every slice of fruit counts as an extra snack in the long run.

Get up and move. Not only will this help you produce endorphins that will help you feel better, but it will also reduce your blood glucose levels. Even if you don't necessarily lose weight with your physical activities, it is still a win for anyone living with diabetes.

Try to get at least two and a half hours of physical activity throughout the week. Be careful to spread that feel-good movement over a couple of days. Never do more than two consecutive days of exercise. Not only will this help prevent injuries, but it will also help you form healthy physical activity habits.

Do you know that you should create a healthy eating plan for your diabetes?
This means you should come up with a nutritional meal plan to follow daily. This will improve your diet and make it healthier.
It would help if you also tried to eat three meals and two snacks daily. This way, you can prevent unhealthy eating habits from developing because this will make it difficult to overeat.
All these tips help you live a healthier lifestyle and enjoy the same time as others without complication.

BREAKFAST

Cheesy Vanilla Crêpe Cakes

Prep time: 5 minutes | Cook time: 20 minutes | Serves 4

Ingredients:

Avocado oil cooking spray
4 ounces (113 g) reduced-fat plain cream cheese, softened 2 medium bananas
4 large eggs
½ teaspoon vanilla extract
⅛ teaspoon salt

Directions:

Heat a large skillet over low heat. Coat the cooking surface with cooking spray, and let the pan heat for another 2 to 3 minutes. Meanwhile, in a medium bowl, mash the cream cheese and bananas together with a fork until combined. The bananas can be a little chunky. Add the eggs, vanilla, and salt, and mix well. For each cake, drop 2 tablespoons of the batter onto the warmed skillet and use the bottom of a large spoon or ladle to spread it thin. Let it cook for 7 to 9 minutes.
Flip the cake over and cook briefly about 1 minute.

Nutrition: calories: 176 | fat: 9.1g | protein: 9.1g | carbs: 15.1g | fiber: 2.1g | sugar: 8.1g | sodium: 214mg

Low Carb Oatmeal Milk Bowl

Prep time: 10 minutes | Cook time: 35 minutes | Serves 6

Ingredients:

2 cups rolled oats
¼ cup shredded unsweetened coconut
1 teaspoon baking powder
½ teaspoon ground cinnamon
¼ teaspoon sea salt
2 cups skim milk
¼ cup melted coconut oil, plus extra for greasing the baking dish 1 egg
1 teaspoon pure vanilla extract
2 cups fresh blueberries
⅛ cup chopped pecans, for garnish

Directions:

1 teaspoon chopped fresh mint leaves, for garnish 1. Preheat the oven to 350ºF (180ºC). Lightly oil a baking dish and set it aside. In a medium bowl, stir together the oats, coconut, baking powder, cinnamon, and salt. Whisk together the milk, oil, egg, and vanilla in a small bowl until well blended. Layer half the dry ingredients in the baking dish, top with half the berries, then spoon the remaining half of the dry ingredients and the rest of the berries on top. Pour the wet ingredients evenly into the baking dish. Tap it lightly on the counter to disperse the wet ingredients throughout. Bake the casserole, uncovered, until the oats are tender, about 35 minutes. Serve immediately, topped with the pecans and mint.

Nutrition: calories: 296 | fat: 17.1g | protein: 10.2g | carbs: 26.9g | fiber: 4.1g | sugar: 10.9g | sodium: 154mg

5 Ingredient Cheese Pancakes with Fruits

Prep time: 10 minutes | Cook time: 20 minutes | Serves 4

Ingredients:
2 cups low-fat cottage cheese
4 egg whites
2 eggs
1 tablespoon pure vanilla extract
1½ cups almond flour
Nonstick cooking spray

Directions:
Place the cottage cheese, egg whites, eggs, and vanilla in a blender and pulse to combine. Add the almond flour to the blender and blend until smooth.
Place a large nonstick skillet over medium heat and lightly coat it with cooking spray. Spoon ¼ cup of batter per pancake, 4 at a time, into the skillet. Cook the pancakes until the bottoms are firm and golden, about 4 minutes. Flip the pancakes over and cook the other side until they are cooked for about 3 minutes. Remove the pancakes to a plate and repeat with the remaining batter.
Serve with fresh fruit.

Nutrition: calories: 345 | fat: 22.1g | protein: 29.1g | carbs: 11.1g | fiber: 4.1g | sugar: 5.1g | sodium: 560mg

Mom's Special Milk Berry Crêpes

Prep time: 20 minutes | Cook time: 20 minutes | Serves 5

Ingredients:
1½ cups skim milk

3 eggs
1 teaspoon extra-virgin olive oil, plus more for the skillet 1 cup buckwheat flour
½ cup whole-wheat flour
½ cup 2 percent low-fat Greek yogurt
1 cup sliced strawberries
1 cup blueberries

Directions:
In a large bowl, whisk together the milk, eggs, and 1 teaspoon of oil until well combined.
Into a medium bowl, sift together the buckwheat and whole-wheat flours.
Add the dry ingredients to the wet ingredients and whisk until well combined and very smooth. Allow the batter to rest for at least 2 hours before cooking. Place a large skillet or crêpe pan over medium-high heat and lightly coat the bottom with oil. Pour about ¼ cup of batter into the skillet. Swirl the pan until the batter completely coats the bottom. Cook the crêpe for about 1 minute, then flip it over—Cook the other side of the crêpe for another minute until lightly browned. Transfer the cooked crêpe to a plate and cover with a clean dish towel to keep warm. Repeat until the batter is used; you should have about 10 crêpes. Spoon 1 tablespoon of yogurt onto each crêpe and place two crêpes on each plate. Top with berries and serve.

Nutrition: calories: 330 | fat: 6.9g | protein: 15.9g | carbs: 54.1g | fiber: 7.9g | sugar: 11.1g | sodium: 100mg

Spiced Spinach Omelet

Prep time: 10 minutes | Cook time: 15 minutes | Serves 4

Ingredients:
2 tablespoons extra-virgin olive oil
½ sweet onion, chopped
1 red bell pepper, seeded and chopped
½ teaspoon minced garlic
¼ teaspoon sea salt
½ teaspoon freshly ground black pepper
8 egg whites
2 cups shredded spinach
½ cup crumbled low-sodium feta cheese
1 teaspoon chopped fresh parsley, for garnish

Directions:
Preheat the oven to 375ºF (190ºC). Place a heavy ovenproof skillet over medium-high heat and add the olive oil. Sauté the onion, bell pepper, and garlic until softened, about 5 minutes.
Season with salt and pepper. Whisk together the egg whites in a medium bowl, pour them into the skillet and lightly shake the pan to disburse.

Cook the vegetables and eggs for 3 minutes without stirring. Scatter the spinach over the eggs and sprinkle the feta cheese evenly over the spinach. Put the skillet in the oven and bake, uncovered, until cooked through and firm, about 10 minutes. Loosen the edges of the frittata with a rubber spatula, then invert it onto a plate. Garnish with the chopped parsley and serve.

Nutrition: calories: 146 | fat: 10.1g | protein: 10.1g | carbs: 3.9g | fiber: 1.0g | sugar: 2.9g | sodium: 292mg

Zucchini Egg Bake

Prep time: 20 minutes | Cook time: 50 minutes | Serves 4

Ingredients:

2 teaspoons extra-virgin olive oil
½ sweet onion, finely chopped
2 teaspoons minced garlic
½ small eggplant, peeled and diced
1 green zucchini, diced
1 yellow zucchini, diced
1 red bell pepper, seeded and diced
3 tomatoes, seeded and chopped
1 tablespoon chopped fresh oregano
1 tablespoon chopped fresh basil
Pinch red pepper flakes
Sea salt and freshly ground black pepper, to taste 4 large eggs.

Directions:

Preheat the oven to 350ºF (180ºC). Place a large ovenproof skillet over medium heat and add the olive oil. Sauté the onion and garlic until softened and translucent, about 3 minutes.
Stir in the eggplant and sauté for about 10 minutes, stirring occasionally.
Stir in the zucchini and pepper and sauté for 5 minutes. Reduce the heat to low and cover. Cook until the vegetables are soft, about 15 minutes. Stir in the tomatoes, oregano, basil, and red pepper flakes, and cook 10 minutes more. Season the ratatouille with salt and pepper. Use a spoon to create four wells in the mixture. Crack an egg into each well. Place the skillet in the oven and bake until the eggs are firm, about 5 minutes. Remove from the oven. Serve the eggs with a generous scoop of vegetables.

Nutritional: calories: 148 | fat: 7.9g | protein: 9.1g | carbs: 13.1g | fiber: 4.1g | sugar: 7.1g | sodium: 99mg

Healthy Whole Wheat Pumpkin Waffles

Prep time: 10 minutes | Cook time: 20 minutes | Serves 6

Ingredients:

2¼ cups whole-wheat pastry flour
2 tablespoons granulated sweetener
1 tablespoon baking powder
1 teaspoon ground cinnamon
1 teaspoon ground nutmeg
4 eggs
1¼ cup pure pumpkin purée
1 apple, peeled, cored, and finely chopped
Melted coconut oil for cooking

Directions:

In a large bowl, stir together the flour, sweetener, baking powder, cinnamon, and nutmeg.
In a small bowl, whisk together the eggs and pumpkin. Add the wet ingredients to the dry and whisk until smooth. Stir the apple into the batter.
Cook the waffles according to the waffle maker's directions, brushing your waffle iron with melted coconut oil until all the batter is gone.
Serve immediately.

Nutrition: calories: 232 | fat: 4.1g | protein: 10.9g | carbs: 40.1g | fiber: 7.1g | sugar: 5.1g | sodium: 52mg

Unique Greek Yogurt Nut Bowl

Prep time: 5 minutes | Cook time: 0 minutes | Serves 2

Ingredients:

1½ cups plain low-fat Greek yogurt
2 kiwis, peeled and sliced
2 tablespoons shredded unsweetened coconut flakes 2 tablespoons halved walnuts
1 tablespoon chia seeds
2 teaspoons honey, divided (optional)

Directions:

Divide the yogurt between two small bowls.
Top each serving of yogurt with half of the kiwi slices, coconut flakes, walnuts, chia seeds, and honey (if using).

Nutrition: calories: 261 | fat: 9.1g | protein: 21.1g | carbs: 23.1g | fiber: 6.1g | sugar: 14.1g | sodium: 84mg

Classic Morning Berry Smoothie

Prep time: 5 minutes | Cook time: 0 minutes | Serves 2

Ingredients:
½ cup mixed berries (blueberries, strawberries, blackberries)
1 tablespoon ground flaxseed
2 tablespoons unsweetened coconut flakes
½ cup unsweetened plain coconut milk
½ cup leafy greens (kale, spinach)
¼ cup unsweetened vanilla nonfat yogurt
½ cup ice

Directions:
Combine the berries, flaxseed, coconut flakes, coconut milk, greens, yogurt, and ice in a blender jar. Process until smooth. Serve.

Nutrition: calories: 182 | fat: 14.9g | protein: 5.9g | carbs: 8.1g | fiber: 4.1g | sugar: 2.9g | sodium: 25mg

Easy Creamy Coconut Kiwi Dessert

Prep time: 5 minutes | Cook time: 0 minutes | Serves 2

Ingredients:
7 ounces (198 g) light coconut milk
¼ cup chia seeds
3 to 4 drops of liquid stevia
1 clementine
1 kiwi
Shredded coconut (unsweetened)

Directions:
Start by taking a mixing bowl and adding the light coconut milk. Add in the liquid stevia to sweeten the milk. Mix well. Add the chia seeds to the milk and whisk until well combined. Set aside. Peel the clementine and carefully remove the skin from the wedges. Set aside. Also, peel the kiwi and dice it into small pieces. Take a glass jar and assemble the pudding. For this, place the fruits at the bottom of the jar; then add a dollop of chia pudding. Now spread the fruits and then add another layer of chia pudding. Finish by garnishing with the remaining fruits and shredded coconut.
Nutrition: calories: 486 | fat: 40.5g | protein: 8.5g | carbs: 30.8g | fiber: 15.6g | sugar: 11.6g | sodium: 24mg

Wheat Apple Bake

Prep time: 10 minutes | Cook time: 20 minutes | Makes 18 muffins

Ingredients:

2 cups whole-wheat flour
1 cup wheat bran
1/3 cup granulated sweetener
1 tablespoon baking powder
2 teaspoons ground cinnamon
½ teaspoon ground ginger
¼ teaspoon ground nutmeg
Pinch sea salt
2 eggs
1½ cups skim milk, at room temperature
½ cup melted coconut oil
2 teaspoons pure vanilla extract
2 apples, peeled, cored, and diced

Directions:

Preheat the oven to 350ºF (180ºC). Line 18 muffin cups with paper liners and set the tray aside. In a large bowl, stir together the flour, bran, sweetener, baking powder, cinnamon, ginger, nutmeg, and salt. Whisk the eggs, milk, coconut oil, and vanilla in a small bowl until blended. Add the wet ingredients to the dry ingredients, stirring until just blended. Stir in the apples and spoon equal batter into each muffin cup. Bake the muffins until a toothpick inserted in the center of a muffin comes out clean, about 20 minutes. Cool the muffins completely and serve. Store leftover muffins in a sealed container in the refrigerator for up to 3 days or in the freezer for up to 1 month.

Nutrition: calories: 142 | fat: 7.1g | protein: 4.1g | carbs: 19.1g | fiber: 3.1g | sugar: 6.1g | sodium: 21mg

Buckwheat Grouts Breakfast Bowl

Prep time: 5 minutes | Cook time: 10-15 minutes | Serves 4

Ingredients:

3 cups skim milk
1 cup buckwheat grouts
¼ cup chia seeds
2 tsp vanilla extract
½tsp ground cinnamon
Pinch salt
1 cup water
½cup unsalted pistachios
2 cups sliced fresh strawberries
¼ cup cacao nibs (optional)

Directions:

In a large bowl, stir together the milk, groats, chia seeds, vanilla, cinnamon, and salt. Cover and refrigerate overnight. The following day, transfer the wet mixture to a medium pot and add the water. Bring to a boil over medium-high heat, reduce the heat to maintain a simmer, and cook for 10–12 minutes until the buckwheat is tender and thickened. Transfer to bowls and serve, topped with the pistachios, strawberries, and cacao nibs (if using).

Nutrition: calories: 340 |total fat: 8 g |saturated fat: 1 g | protein: 15 g | carbs: 52 g | sugar: 14 g fiber: 10 g | cholesterol: 4 mg | sodium: 140 mg

Steel-Cut Oatmeal Bowl with Fruit and Nuts

Prep time: 5 minutes | Cook time: 20 minutes | Serves 4

Ingredients:

1 cup steel-cut oats
2 cups almond milk
¾ cup water
1 tsp ground cinnamon
¼ tsp salt
2 cups chopped fresh fruit, such as blueberries, strawberries, raspberries, or peaches
½cup chopped walnuts
¼ cup chia seeds

Directions:

In a medium saucepan over medium-high heat, combine the oats, almond milk, water, cinnamon, and salt. Bring to a boil, reduce the heat to low, and simmer for 15–20 minutes until the oats are softened and thickened. Top each bowl with ½cup of fresh fruit, 2 tbsp walnuts, and 1 tbsp chia seeds before serving.

Nutrition: calories: 288 | total fat: 11 g | saturated fat: 1 g | protein: 10 g | carbs: 38 g | sugar: 7 g fiber: 10 g | cholesterol: 0 mg | sodium: 329 mg

Breakfast Pita Bacon with Pepper

Prep time: 5 minutes | Cook time: 15 minutes | Serves 2

Ingredients:

1 (6-inch) whole-grain pita bread
3 teaspoons extra-virgin olive oil, divided
2 eggs
2 Canadian bacon slices
Juice of ½ lemons

1 cup micro greens
2 tablespoons crumbled goat cheese
Freshly ground black pepper, to taste

Directions:
Heat a large skillet over medium heat. Cut the pita bread in half and brush each side of both halves with ¼ teaspoon olive oil (1 teaspoon oil). Cook for 2 to 3 minutes on each side, then remove from the skillet. In the same skillet, heat 1 teaspoon of oil over medium heat. Crack the eggs into the skillet and cook until the eggs are set, 2 to 3 minutes. Remove from the skillet. In the same skillet, cook the Canadian bacon for 3 to 5 minutes, flipping once. Whisk the remaining 1 teaspoon of oil and lemon juice in a large bowl. Add the micro greens and toss to combine. Top each pita half with half of the microgreens, 1 piece of bacon, 1 egg, and 1 tablespoon of goat cheese. Season with pepper and serve.

Nutrition: calories: 251 | fat: 13.9g | protein: 13.1g | carbs: 20.1g | fiber: 3.1g | sugar: 0.9g | sodium: 400mg

Vegetarian Lentils with Egg Toast

Prep time: 15 minutes | Cook time: 10 minutes | Serves 2

Ingredients:
2 ounces low-sodium vegetable broth
1 medium onion, diced
2 cloves garlic, minced
½ yellow bell pepper, sliced
½ red bell pepper, sliced
½ orange bell pepper, sliced
One 15-ounce can of low-sodium canned lentils, drained
½ teaspoon smoked paprika
⅛teaspoon chipotle powder
½ teaspoon garlic powder
Ground black pepper to taste
Olive-oil spray
2 large eggs
2 slices of whole-grain bread
2 Tablespoons fresh parsley, torn
¼ avocado, sliced
½ lemon, sliced

Directions:
Cook onions and garlic in vegetable stock in a large sauté pan over medium-high heat until transparent, stirring periodically. Cook for 3-4 minutes, stirring periodically, with the bell peppers. In a mixing bowl, combine lentils, paprika, chipotle powder, garlic powder, and black pepper. Reduce the

heat to medium and simmer for 3-4 minutes, stirring regularly. Meanwhile, cut a hole in each piece of bread with a plain-edged tiny circular cutter; toast the bread. Spray a medium frying pan with oil and cook the eggs upside down. Divide the lentil mixture into two dishes and top with an egg and a slice of bread with the hole over the yolk. Top each platter with parsley and garnish with avocado and lemon. Squeeze the juice of a lemon slice over the lentil mixture.
Nutrition: calories: 319 | fat: 2.9g | protein: 4.1g | carbs: 0g | fiber: 2.8g | sugar: 1.9g | sodium: 64mg

High Protein Oatmeal

Prep time: 5 minutes | Cook time: 10 minutes | Serves 1

Ingredients:
3/4 cup rolled oats
2 eggs
1/2 cup milk
1 Tablespoon ground flaxseed
1 teaspoon cinnamon
1 ripe banana, mashed

Directions:
In a saucepan over medium-high heat, combine all the ingredients. Cook, often stirring, until the mixture reaches the consistency of typical oatmeal and the eggs are no longer runny. This will take around 5 minutes.
Nutrition: calories: 325 | fat: 2.9g | protein: 26g | carbs: 49g | fiber: 8g | sugar: 11g | sodium: 206mg

Healthy Bagel Toppings

Prep time: 5 minutes | Serves: 1

Ingredients:
2 whole-wheat mini bagels
3 large eggs
1/4 cup shredded mozzarella cheese
2 links chicken breakfast sausages
Salt and black pepper to taste
FOR THE SPINACH AND MUSHROOM BAGELS:
2 whole-wheat mini bagels
1 teaspoon extra-virgin olive oil
2 cups fresh spinach
4 oz. cremini or white button mushrooms, sliced
2 large eggs
Salt and black pepper to taste
2 whole-wheat mini bagels

2 oz. cream cheese
A handful of assorted berries: strawberries, blueberries, blackberries
Drizzle of honey
2 whole-wheat mini bagels
3 tablespoons peanut butter
1 small banana, sliced
Sprinkle of chia seeds
Drizzle of honey

Directions:
Spray a pan with nonstick cooking spray and heat over medium-low heat. In a small mixing bowl, crack the eggs and whisk with a fork until thoroughly blended. Add a splash of water, season with salt and pepper, and whisk once more. Pour eggs into the pan and simmer over medium-low heat, turning periodically until cooked. When the eggs are almost done, add the cheese and stir to mix—season with salt and pepper to taste. Meanwhile, cook the chicken sausages until heated and slightly browned in a small skillet over medium heat. Transfer to a cutting board and cut. (Once the eggs are mostly cooked, you may heat them in the same pan as the eggs.) Push them to the side to create room.) Fill each bagel half with cheesy scrambled eggs and sausage pieces. Serve immediately—bagels with spinach and mushrooms. Toast the bagels. In a large skillet over medium heat, heat the olive oil. Sauté the mushrooms until most of the liquid has been taken out and evaporated—season with salt and pepper to taste after adding the spinach. Stir in the spinach until it is almost wilted. Push the vegetables to the side and crack the eggs into the pan. (If preferred, spray with nonstick cooking spray or add a little additional olive oil or butter.) Fry the eggs until they are done to your liking. (If you want, you may flip them over to cook the tops.) You may also place a lid on the pan to assist the top's cooking/steam a little more.) Season with salt and pepper to taste. Pile spinach and mushrooms on either side of a bagel, then top with a cooked egg. Season with salt and pepper to taste, and serve hot—bagels with cream cheese and fruit Toast the bagels. Spread cream cheese on each side of a bagel. Drizzle with honey and top with various berries.
Nutrition: calories: 227 | fat: 2.9g | protein: 8 | carbs: 49g | fiber: 6g | sugar: 9g | sodium: 323mg

Cinnamon Walnut Breakfast Bowl

Prep time: 5 minutes | Cook time: 30 minutes | Serves 4

Ingredients:
4 cups rolled oats
1 cup walnut pieces
½ cup pepitas
¼ teaspoon salt
1 teaspoon ground cinnamon
1 teaspoon ground ginger ½ cup coconut oil, melted
½ cup unsweetened applesauce
1 teaspoon vanilla extract

½ cup dried cherries

Directions:
Preheat the oven to 350ºF (180ºC). Line a baking sheet with parchment paper. In a large bowl, toss the oats, walnuts, pepitas, salt, cinnamon, and ginger: mix coconut oil, applesauce, and vanilla in a large measuring cup. Pour over the dry mixture and mix well. Transfer the mixture to the prepared baking sheet. Cook for 30 minutes, stirring about halfway through. Remove from the oven and let the granola sit undisturbed until completely cool. Break the granola into pieces and stir in the dried cherries. Transfer to an airtight container, and store at room temperature for up to 2 weeks.
Nutrition: calories: 194 | fat: 5g | protein: 14 | carbs: 11g | fiber: 6g

Vanilla flavored Berry Muffins

Prep time: 20 minutes | Cook time: 25 minutes | Serves 18

Ingredients:
2 cups whole-wheat pastry flour
1 cup almond flour
½ cup granulated sweetener
1 tablespoon baking powder
2 teaspoons freshly grated lemon zest
¾ teaspoon baking soda
¾ teaspoon ground nutmeg
Pinch sea salt
2 eggs
1 cup skim milk, at room temperature
¾ cup 2 percent low-fat Greek yogurt
½ cup melted coconut oil
1 tablespoon freshly squeezed lemon juice
1 teaspoon pure vanilla extract
1 cup fresh blueberries

Directions:
Preheat the oven to 350ºF (180ºC). Line 18 muffin cups with paper liners and set the tray aside. In a large bowl, stir together the flour, almond flour, sweetener, baking powder, lemon zest, baking soda, nutmeg, and salt. Whisk together the eggs, milk, yogurt, coconut oil, lemon juice, and vanilla in a small bowl. Add the wet ingredients to the dry ingredients and stir until just combined. Fold in the blueberries without crushing them. Spoon the batter evenly into the muffin cups. Bake the muffins until a toothpick inserted in the middle comes out clean, about 25 minutes. Cool the muffins completely and serve. Store leftover muffins in a sealed container in the refrigerator for up to 3 days or in the freezer for up to 1 month.
Nutrition: calories: 657 | fat: 15g | protein: 47 | carbs: 71g | fiber: 16g

Perfectly Poached Eggs

Prep time: 10 minutes | **Cook time:** 5 minutes | **Serves:** 2

Ingredients:
2 large fresh eggs
Few drops of distilled vinegar
Pinch of sea salt

Directions:
Water to boil. Crack the eggs and add a few drops of distilled vinegar. Boil the water in a pan and stir it in a circular motion. Add the eggs to the water as it's swirling and turn off the heat. Leave it there for 4 to 5 minutes and lift it with a slotted spoon. Sprinkle with sea salt.
Nutrition: calories: 47 | fat: 3.5g | protein: 7g | carbs: 12g | sodium 88mg

Perfectly Scrambled Eggs

Prep time: 10 minutes | Cook time: 5 minutes | Serves: 2

Ingredients:
9 Eggs
1 ½ tbsp. Butter, cold and cut into cubes
1 ½ tbsp. Crème Fraiche
Pinch of sea salt

Directions:
Break the eggs and add the butter Stir over medium heat until it starts to cook. Remove from heat and continue stirring. Return to the heat and continue stirring. Continue this until the butter begins to clump. As soon as they tread, add the crème Fraiche and return to the heat. Remove from heat while the eggs are soft, slightly runny, and clumpy. Add sea salt to taste.
Nutrition: calories: 207 | fat: 15.5g | protein: 17g | carbs: 16g | sodium 6mg

Perfectly Boiled Eggs

Prep time: 10 minutes | Cook time: 6 minutes | Serves 4

Ingredients:
3 large eggs
3 pinches of salt

Directions:
Fill a small saucepan with room temperature water. Add the egg.s Bring water to a boil over maximum heat and cover with a glass lid. Remove the pan from the heat as water starts to bubble. Keep the top on. Take the eggs out of the water after 6 minutes.

Nutrition: calories: 77 | total fat: 7 g | saturated fat: 1.6 g | protein: 6.3 g | carbs: 0.6 g | cholesterol: 215 mg

Smoothie with Greek Yogurt and Berries for Breakfast

Prep Time: 5 minutes | Cook Time: 0 minutes | Servings: 1

Ingredients:
1 cup of mixed berries (frozen)
1 cup without fat strained Greek yogurt
2 tbsp. of milk with no fat or tart juice of any kind like cranberry, pomegranate or cherry
1 tbsp. sweetener with choice

Directions:
Put all the ingredients in your blender, blend it until it gets smooth.

Nutrition: Carbs: 30g | Proteins: 22g | Fats: 0g

Blueberry Muffins of Whole-Wheat having Protein

Prep Time: 5 minutes | Cook time: 25mins | Servings: 2

Ingredients:
2 cups of blueberries
1 tablespoon of baking powder
3 cups + 1 tablespoon of flour (whole wheat), separated ½ tablespoon of baking soda
10 tablespoons of softened butter
2 eggs
1 tablespoon zest of lemon
1 tablespoon extract of vanilla
1½ cups yogurt

Directions:
Put the racks of oven in lower-middle part in the oven. Oven should be preheated at 375°F. Grease every muffin cup separately and Set it aside.
Toss the blueberries and mix in a medium kind of bowl; before mixing, put 1 tablespoon flour and Set aside.
Whisk flour, baking soda and baking powder together in another bowl and leave aside.
Beat sugar and cream butter together in a mixing bowl until it gets fluffy.
Eggs should be added one by one, beat it until it gets well mixed, and lemon zest and vanilla should contain also be mixed, and beating is done.
Make sure that beating is done for just incorporation. Half of the ingredients, which are dry, should be beaten until they get mixed. Beat ½ cup of plain yogurt. And beat remaining dry ingredients. Beat in the ½ cup of your yogurt.
Beat dry ingredients which are left, then after that the yogurt. Wrap it in berries.

With a scoop of ice cream, put equal muffin dough in the cups but for bigger muffins, put some dough to fill until cups become nearly full and to make a small muffin, it should fill till 3/4 to full.
Bake for about 30 minutes, so the muffins become golden brown, and the toothpick which was inserted into the muffin comes out as clean.

Nutrition: Carbs: 27.4g | Protein: 3.6g | Fat: 4.6g

Cereal of Whole-Grain with Oatmeal, Ground Flaxseed and Eggs

Prep time: 2 min | Cook time: 5 min | Servings: 2

Ingredients:
3/4 cup of rolled oats
1 tbsp. of cinnamon
1/2 cup of milk
2 eggs
1 tbsp. of ground flaxseed
1 mashed ripe banana

Directions:
Incorporate all ingredients in a pot turn the stove to high medium flame.
Cook it and stir it frequently so that the mixture becomes a normal oatmeal type of consistency and eggs are longer no runny. It will have five minutes.

Nutrition: Carbs: 5.3g | Protein: 10.9g | Fat: 17.2g

Vegetarian Lentils and Eggs on a Toast

Prep Time: 5 min | Cook Time: 10 min | Servings: 1

Ingredients:
2-ounce vegetable broth with low-sodium
2 minced cloves of garlic
1 medium diced onion
½ yellow sliced bell pepper
½ orange sliced bell pepper
½ red sliced bell pepper
1 drained 15-ounce canned lentils with low-sodium ⅛ tbsp. powder chipotle
½ tbsp. paprika, which is smoked
½ tbsp. powder garlic
2 eggs
Grounded black pepper of your preference
2 tbsp. of fresh parsley, which is torn
Spray of olive-oil
½ sliced lemon

2 slices of whole grained bread
¼ sliced avocado

Directions:

In vegetable broth, cook garlic and onions in a large pan over medium to high heat until they become translucent and stir it time to time.

Cook it for 3 to 4 minutes after adding bell peppers. Also, stir it from time to time. Mix in chipotle powder, lentils, black pepper, garlic powder, and paprika.

Reduce the heat flame to medium, and cook it for 3-4 min and stir it frequently. In that time, cut out the hole in every piece of the bread for this use plain edge type of small cutter which is round and the bread should be toasted.

The frying pan is coated with a medium through spray oil, cook eggs.

Separate the lentil mixture into two plates, and topping is done of each through an egg, then slice the toast with the hole over the yolk of the egg.

Parsley is sprinkled on top and garnishes the plate with lemon and avocado.

Squeeze the juice of the lemon on the lentil mixture.

Nutrition: Carbs: 6g| Protein: 5g| Fat: 2g

Breakfast Burritos Mushroom Freezer

Prep time: 15 min| cook time: 30 min | servings: 2

Ingredients:

2 tbsp. of neutral oil vegetable, grapeseed, canola ½ diced white onion
2 minced garlic clove
2 cups chopped crimini type mushrooms
4 cups chopped spinach which is packed loosely
¼ tsp of salt
8 eggs
3 tbsp. milk
pepper and salt according to taste
spray for Cooking
4 large tortillas of whole wheat
¼ cup and 2 tbsp. of goat cheese
Substitutions and Swaps Ingredient
Goat cheese, feta cheese or mozzarella cheese

Directions:

Cook mushrooms till it is golden brown. Put spinach in the skillet to cook it until it gets wilted. Season it in salt, then remove it from the heat and put it aside.

Make a mixture by whisking the eggs & milk, then season it with pepper and salt.

Cook the mixture of eggs in the different skillet when the eggs are set, then it should be removed from the stove.

The tortillas should be heated in a microwave oven, then lay tortillas on 4

different foil pieces. Goat cheese should be spread on every tortilla. Add vegetables that are roasted and also the eggs which are scrambled. Roll it up in aluminum foil, then place it in the bag for freezing put it in freezer.
When it becomes ready for eating, put it out of the freezer, then burritos should be unwrapped from aluminum foil and then microwave to heat it throughout.

Nutrition: Carbs: 41.0g, Protein: 21.1g, Fat: 12.5g

Zucchini White Cheddar Muffins

Prep Time 10 mins| Cook Time 25 mins | Servings: 2

Ingredients:
1¼ cup flour of almond
3 eggs
½ teaspoon of baking soda
¼ teaspoon of coarse salt
¼ teaspoon of black pepper
½ teaspoon of onion powder
½ teaspoon of garlic powder
1 cup + 1 Tablespoon of cheddar cheese, which is shredded 1 cup squeezed zucchini which is shredded

Directions:
Oven should be preheated to 350°F.
Pulse in a blender the flour, baking soda, eggs and spices until it gets smooth.
Add the zucchini and 1 cup of cheese. Pulse the mixture till the zucchini get completely incorporated; note it that it should not get pureed. You could still see flecks of the green in the throughout batter.
Then spoon all the batter in a lined type of muffin tins; it should be 3/4 full.
The topping should be done with 1 Tablespoon of cheese. Then Bake it at 350°F for 25 min until all muffins get golden, and the pre-inserted toothpick in muffins clean comes out.
After 3 to 5 min when muffins get cooled enough that they can be touched, take out muffins from the pan and cool them on the cooling rack and Serve it warm.

Nutrition: Carbs: 5g, Protein: 10g, Fat: 15g

Grits of Scallion with Shrimp

Prep time 15min| Cook time 20min | Servings 6

Ingredients:
1 ½ cups milk which is fat-free
2 leaves of bay
1 ½ cups of water
1 cup of corn grits, which is stone ground

¼ Cup Broth of Seafood
2 thinly sliced scallions, green and white parts
2 minced garlic cloves
1 pound shelled & deveined medium-size shrimp ½ tsp paprika, which is smoked
½ dried dill tsp
¼ tsp seeds of celery

Directions:
Use a medium-size stockpot, mix the milk, bay leaves and water, then bring it to boil on high flame.
Put in the grits in a Gradual manner and stir it continuously.
Decrease the heat, cover and then cook it for 5-7 min, stirs it often and till grits become soft. Remove from the heat and discard the bay leaves.
Use a small skillet of cast iron and take the broth to simmer on medium flame.
Scallions and garlic should be added and sauté it for 3-5 min to make it softened.
Then celery seeds, paprika, shrimp and dill were added after it got cooked for approx. 7-8 min and when the shrimp became light pink not cooked over.
Plate every dish for about ¼ cup with grits and top it with the shrimp.
The size of one serving is about ¼ cup of grits and about 4-5 shrimp in a serving

Nutrition: Carbs: 25g, Protein: 20g, Fat: 1g

Berry Yogurt Bowl

Prep time 5min| Cook time 5min | Servings 1

Ingredients:
3/4 cup of plain type of Greek yogurt (2%)
1 tablespoon of mint which is Chopped
2 1/2 tablespoon walnuts chopped
1/2 cup of Citrus also Mint Berries

Directions:
Put the yogurt in the bowl. Mint Berries, walnuts, Citrus and mint Topping, are done.
Eat it fresh, and you can keep it chilled.

Nutrition: Carbs: 35g, Protein: 25g, Fat: 9 g

Classic Omelet & Greens

Prep Time: 5mins | Cook Time: 15mins | Servings: 1

Ingredients:
1 chopped yellow onion
3 tablespoons of olive oil
3 ounces of baby spinach
8 large-sized eggs
2 tablespoons butter, unsalted

2 tablespoons of lemon juice
Kosher salt
1 ounce of grated Parmesan

Directions:
In a big saucepan, heat 1 tbsp. oil on moderate flame. Add the onion and cook for approximately 5 min, or until it is soft. Place in a mixing bowl. Mix together eggs, 1 tbsp. water, and 1/2 tsp salt in a large mixing dish. Return the skillet to medium-high heat and add the butter. Cook continuously, whisking with a spatula, until the eggs are partially set. Lower the heat and simmer for 5 - 6 minutes, or till eggs are set. Fold it in half & sprinkle with Parmesan as well as fried onion. Mix together the lime juice and the leftover 2 tbsp. oil in a mixing bowl. Mix the spinach with some vinaigrette before serving with the omelet.

Nutrition: Carbs: 6g, Protein: 16g, Fat: 27.5g

Overnight Chilled Chia

Prep Time: 20mins | Cook Time: 0mins | Servings: 3

Ingredients:
4 tablespoon of chia seeds
2 cup of oats, old-fashioned
4 tablespoon of honey
Blueberry-Coconut
Milk
4 tablespoon of chia seeds
3 cups of coconut milk
4 tablespoon of honey
1 teaspoon of lemon zest
4 tablespoon of cocoa powder, Unsweetened
blueberries
Sliced strawberries
4 tablespoon of hazelnut-chocolate spread
PB&J
toasted hazelnuts, chopped
4 tablespoon of Strawberry jam
4 cup of oats, old-fashioned
milk
4 tablespoon of honey
4 tablespoons of peanut butter

Directions:
Add half cup oats, 1 tbsp. seeds chia, 1 tbsp. honey and 2/3 part of milk to each one of 4 (16-oz) jars. Cover and give it a good shake to incorporate everything. Chill or refrigerate. Add half cup of oats, 1 tbsp. Chia seed, and also 1 tbsp. of honey and about 3/4 cup of coconut milk to every one of four 16

ounces' jars. Refrigerate after covering with plastic wrap and shaking to mix. For serving, put 1/4 tbsp. lemon zest and top each jar with some blueberries.
Combine a half cup of oats, 1 tbsp. Seeds of chia, 1 tbsp. Honey, milk and 1
tbsp. Chocolate powder in four jars of 16 oz. Refrigerate after covering with plastic wrap and shaking to mix. Mix 1 tbsp. chocolate and hazelnut spread within every jar once it has been soaked, then sprinkle with some hazelnuts.
Put half cup oats, 1 tbsp. Seeds of chia, 1 tbsp. of honey and 2/3 of milk to every four 16-oz jars for PB and J. Refrigerate after covering with plastic wrap and shaking to mix. After being soaked, mix in 1 tbsp. peanut butter as well as top every jar with a tbsp. jam of strawberry and some strawberries.
Nutrition: Carbs: 57g, Protein: 12g, Fat: 12g

Berry Oatmeal

Prep Time: 5mins | Cook Time: 0mins | Servings: 3

Ingredients:
1/2 cup of Mint and Citrus Berries
1/2 cup of Easy and Quick Oatmeal 1 1/2 tablespoon of walnuts

Directions:
Quick and Easy Oatmeal is reheated. Citrus with berries of mint, as well as walnuts, go on the topping.

Nutrition: Carbs: 23.4 g, Protein: 5.8g, Fat: 2.8g

LUNCH

Chicken with Peach-Avocado Salsa

Prep time: 25 minutes | Serves 4

Ingredients:
Medium peach 1
Ripe avocado 1 medium
Red pepper 1/2 cup of
Red onion 3 tbsp
Fresh basil 1 tbsp
Lime juice 1 tbsp
Pepper sauce 1 tsp
Lime zest 1/2 tsp
Salt 3/4 tsp
Pepper 1/2 tsp

Chicken breast 4 boneless

Directions:
Mix peaches, lime juice, 1/4 tsp of pepper, avocado, red pepper, onion, basil, lime zest, 1/4 tsp of salt, & spicy sauce inside the small bowl to form salsa. Add the remaining salt & pepper to the chicken. Grill chicken for 5mins, covered, on the lightly oiled grill rack on moderate flame. Turn and cook for another 7-9 mins, till the thermometer registers 165°. Serve with a side of salsa.

Nutrition: calories 199 kcal| protein 4.2g| carbohydrates 8.6g|fat 9.8g

Pressure-Cooker Italian Shrimp 'n' Pasta

Prep time: 20 minutes | Serves 6

Ingredients:
2 tbsp canola oil
1 lb skinless chicken boneless
1 can of tomatoes crushed
1-1/2 cups of water
2 chopped celery ribs
1 green pepper medium
1 coarsely chopped medium onion
2 minced garlic cloves
1 tbsp sugar
½ tsp salt
½ tsp Italian seasoning
¼ tsp pepper cayenne
1 leaf bay
1 cup of orzo uncooked
1 lb cooked shrimp peeled & deveined

Directions:
In a 6-quart pressure cooker, choose the saute mode, then set the temperature to medium. 1 tsp of oil Brown the chicken through batches once the oil is heated, adding more oil as required. To cancel, use the cancel button. In a large mixing bowl, combine the following 11 components. Close the release valve and lock the lid. Adjust on high pressure and cook for approximately 8 mins. The pressure that releases quickly. To cancel, use the cancel button. Bay leaf should be discarded. Select the saute option & set the temperature to medium. Toss in the orzo. Cook till the pasta is al dente, turning often. Stir in the shrimp and cook for another 2 mins, or till cooked through. To cancel, use the cancel button.

Nutrition: calories: 450 kcal | fats: 21 g | proteins: 17.7 g | carbohydrates: 47 g

Curried Chicken Skillet

Prep time: 30 minutes | Serves 4

Ingredients:
Chicken broth 1-1/3 cups of
Quinoa rinsed, 2/3 cup of
Canola oil 1 tbsp
Sweet potato 1 medium
Medium onion 1
Celery rib chopped 1
Frozen peas 1 cup of
Garlic cloves 2
Fresh ginger root 1 tsp
Curry powder 3 tsp
Salt 1/4 tsp
Cooked chicken

Directions:
Bring 1-1/3 cup broth to a boil inside the small saucepan. Toss in the quinoa. Reduce heat to low and cook, covered, for 12-15 mins, or till the liquid has absorbed. Cook potato, onion, and celery inside the large pan on moderate-high heat until potatoes are cooked, about 10-12 mins. Cook & stir for 2 mins with peas, garlic, ginger, & spices. Heat through the chicken and the leftover broth. Add the quinoa and mix well.

Nutrition: calories 179 kcal| protein 9.4g| carbohydrates 6.6g|fat 5.8g

Chicken & Spanish Cauliflower "Rice."

Prep time: 30 minutes | Serves 4

Ingredients:
1 large cauliflower head
1 lb chicken breasts boneless skinless
½ tsp salt
½ tsp pepper
1 tbsp canola oil
2 medium chopped green pepper
1 chopped small onion
1 minced garlic clove
½ cup of juice tomato
¼ tsp cumin ground
¼ cup of fresh cilantro chopped

1 tbsp juice lime

Directions:
Cauliflower should be cored and sliced into 1-inch pieces. Inside the food processor, chop cauliflower throughout batches till it looks like rice. Season the chicken using salt & pepper before serving. Heat oil inside the large pan on moderate-high heat and cook the chicken until it is nicely browned, approximately 5 minutes. Cook & stir for 3 mins after adding the green pepper, onion, & garlic. Bring to a boil, stirring in the tomato juice & cumin. Cook over moderate flame for 7-10 mins, or till cauliflower is cooked, stirring occasionally. Add the cilantro & lime juice to mix well.

Nutrition: calories: 250 kcal | fats: 21 g | proteins: 17.7 g | carbohydrates: 47 g

Coconut Flour Tortillas

Prep time: 10 minutes | Cook time: 15 minutes | Serves 4

Ingredients:
3/4 cup egg whites
1/3 cup water
1/4 cup coconut flour
1 tsp. sunflower oil
1/2 tsp. salt
1/2 tsp. cumin
1/2 tsp. chili powder
Directions:
Add all the ingredients, except oil, to a food processor and pulse until combined. Let rest for 7–8 minutes. Heat the oil in a large skillet over med-low heat. Pour 1/4 cup batter into the center and tilt to spread to 7–8-inch circle. When the top is no longer shiny, flip the tortilla and cook for 1–2 minutes. Repeat with the remaining batter. Place each tortilla on parchment paper and lightly wipe off excess oil.

Nutrition: calories: 26.5 | carbs: 0.9g | protein: 5.3g | fat: 0g | sugar: 0g | fiber: 0g

Turkey Escalope Pan

Prep time: 8 hours 35 minutes | Cook time: 30 minutes | Serves 2

Ingredients:
11.3 ounces potatoes
3.52 ounces carrots
10 ounces pointed cabbage
2 turkey schnitzel
2 slices of Emmental

4 tbsp oil
150 ml vegetable broth

Directions:
Peel the potatoes and cut them into small cubes. Peel the carrots. Wash the cabbage and shake it dry. Cut both into small pieces. Prepare the vegetable stock. Peel the onion and cut it into small cubes. Wash turkey schnitzel, dab it and fry in a pan with hot oil for 5–10 minutes.
Turn in half the time. Remove turkey from heat and keep warm.
Sauté the onions in a pan with hot. Add the potatoes and carrots and fry briefly. Deglaze with the vegetable stock. Put a lid on the pot and cook everything for ¼ hour. After about 5 minutes, add the cabbage. Mix well. Season with salt and pepper and then serve.

Nutrition: calories: 250 | fat: 7.0 g | protein: 25.0 g

Chickpea Soup

Prep time: 15 minutes | Cook time: 35 minutes | Serves 2

Ingredients:
1 lb. cooked chickpeas
1 lb. vegetables, chopped
1 cup low-sodium vegetable broth
2 tbsp. mixed herbs

Directions:
Mix all the ingredients in an instant pot. Cook on STEW for 35 minutes. Release the pressure naturally.

Nutrition: calories: 309.8 | carbs: 19.8g | sugar: 2.8g | fat: 4.7g | protein: 27.3g

Classic Stroganoff

Prep time: 15 minutes | Cook time: 20 minutes | Serves 5

Ingredients:
5 oz (142 g) cooked egg noodles
2 tsp olive oil
1 lb (454 g) beef tenderloin tips, boneless, sliced into 2-inch strips 1 ½cups white button mushrooms, sliced
½cup onion, minced
1 tbsp all-purpose flour

½cup dry white wine
1 (14.5 oz/411 g) can of fat-free, low-sodium beef broth 1 tsp Dijon mustard
½cup fat-free sour cream
¼tsp salt
¼tsp black pepper

Directions:
Put the cooked egg noodles on a large plate. Warmth the olive oil. Add the beef and sauté for 3 minutes or until lightly browned. Detach the beef from the skillet and set it on the plate with noodles. Add the mushrooms and onion to the skillet and sauté for 5 minutes or until tender and the onion browns. Add the flour and cook for a minute. Add the white wine and cook for 2
more minutes. Add the beef broth and Dijon mustard. Bring to a boil. Keep stirring. Reduce the heat to low and simmer for another 5 minutes.
Attach the beef back to the skillet and simmer for an additional 3 minutes.
Add the remaining ingredients and simmer for 1 minute.
Pour them over the egg noodles and beef and serve immediately.

Nutrition: calories: 275 | fat: 7.0 g

Pork Chops with Apples and Red Cabbage

Prep time: 15 minutes | Cook time: 30 minutes | Serves 4

Ingredients:
¼ cup apple cider vinegar
2 tablespoons granulated sweetener
4 (4-ounce) pork chops, about 1 inch thick
1 tablespoon extra-virgin olive oil
½ red cabbage, finely shredded
1 sweet onion, thinly sliced
1 apple, peeled, cored, and sliced
1 teaspoon chopped fresh thyme

Direction:
Scourge together the vinegar and sweetener. Set it aside. Season the pork with salt and
pepper. Position a huge skillet over medium-high heat and add the olive oil. Cook the pork chops until no longer pink, turning once, about 8 minutes per side. Put chops aside. Add the cabbage and onion to the skillet and sauté until the vegetables have softened about 5 minutes. Add the vinegar mixture and the apple slices to the skillet and bring the mixture to a boil. Reduce heat to low and simmer, covered, for 5 additional minutes. Return the pork chops to the skillet, along with any accumulated juices and thyme, cover, and cook for 5 minutes.

Nutrition: calories: 222.7 | carbs: 11.3g | fiber: 3g | protein: 23.0 g | carbs: 29.0 g | fiber: 4.0 g | sugar: 3.0 g | sodium: 250 mg

Pressure-Cooker Pork Tacos with Mango Salsa

Prep time: 25 minutes | Serves 12

Ingredients:
white vinegar 2 tbsp
lime juice 2 tbsp
fresh pineapple 3 cups of
red onion 1 small
chili powder 3 tbsp
chipotle peppers 2
ground cumin 2 tsp
salt 1-1/2 tsp
pepper 1/2 tsp
Mexican beer 1 bottle
pork tenderloin 3 lb
fresh cilantro 1/4 cup chopped
Mango salsa 1 jar (16 oz)(450 gr)
corn tortillas 24

Directions:
Inside the blender, puree the first nine ingredients; whisk within the beer. Combine the meat & pineapple mix in a 6-quart pressure cooker. Close the release valve and lock the lid. Adjust on high pressure and cook for approximately 3 mins. The force that releases quickly. A thermometer put into pork should register a temperature of at least 145°F(62°C). To split up the meat, stir it around. Toss the cilantro into the salsa. Serve pork mix in tortillas with the slotted spoon; sprinkle with salsa & garnishes as desired.

Nutrition: calories 189 kcal | protein 9.2g | carbohydrates 3.6g | fat 8.8g

Ritzy Beef Stew

Prep time: 20 minutes | Cook time: 2 hours | Serves 4

Ingredients:
2 tbsp all-purpose flour
1 tbsp Italian seasoning
2 lb (907 g) top round, cut into ¾-inch cubes
2 tbsp olive oil
4 cups low-sodium chicken broth, divided

1 ½lb (680 g) Cremini mushrooms, rinsed, stems removed, and quartered
1 large onion, coarsely chopped
3 garlic cloves, minced
3 medium carrots, peeled and cut into ½-inch pieces 1 cup frozen peas
1 tbsp fresh thyme, minced
1 tbsp red wine vinegar
½tsp freshly ground black pepper

Directions:
Combine the flour and Italian seasoning in a large bowl. Dredge the beef cubes in the bowl to coat well. Heat the olive oil in a pot over medium heat until shimmering. Add the beef to the single layer in the pot and cook for 2–4 minutes or until golden brown on all sides. Flip the beef cubes frequently. Detach the beef from the pot, set it aside, and add ¼ cup of chicken broth to the bank. Add the mushrooms and sauté for 4 minutes or until soft. Remove the mushrooms from the pot and set them aside. Set ¼ cup of chicken broth in the pot. Add the onions and garlic to the bank and sauté for 4 minutes or until translucent.
Put the beef back into the pot and pour the remaining broth. Bring to a boil. Reduce the heat to low and cover. Simmer for 45 minutes. Stir periodically. Add the carrots, mushroom, peas, and thyme to the pot and simmer for 45 more minutes or until the vegetables are soft. Open the lid, drizzle with red wine vinegar, and season with black pepper.
Stir and serve in a large bowl.
Nutrition: calories: 250 | fat: 7.0 g | protein: 25.0 g | carbs: 24.0 g | fiber: 3.0 g | sugar: 5.0 g | sodium: 290 mg

Beer Bread

Prep time: 5 minutes | Cook time: 45 minutes | Serves 14

Ingredients:
1/4 cup butter, soft
12 oz. light beer
3 cup low-carb baking mix
1/3 cup Splenda

Directions:
Heat oven to 375ºF (190°C). Use 1 tbsp of butter to grease the bottom of a 9x5-inch loaf pan. Whisk together baking mix, beer, and Splenda in a large bowl. Pour into the prepared pan. Bake for 45 minutes. Cool in pan 10 minutes, remove from pan, and cool on wire rack. Melt the remaining butter in a microwave and brush over a warm loaf in a small glass bowl; cool for 15 minutes before slicing.

Nutrition: calories: 161.7 | carbs: 15.9g | protein: 9.3g | fat: 4.9g | sugar: 4.6g | fiber: 4g

Slow Cooked Beef and Vegetables Roast

Prep time: 15 minutes | Cook time: 4 hours | Serves 4

Ingredients:
1 tbsp olive oil
2 medium celery stalks, halved lengthwise and cut into 3-inch pieces 4 medium carrots, scrubbed, halved lengthwise, and cut into 3-inch pieces
1 medium onion, cut in eighths
1¼lb (567 g) lean chuck roast, boneless, trimmed of fat 2 tsp Worcestershire sauce
1 tbsp balsamic vinegar
2 tbsp water
1 tbsp onion soup mix
½tsp ground black pepper

Directions:
Grease a Slow Cooker with olive oil. Set the celery, carrots, and onion in the Slow Cooker, then add the beef. Top them with Worcestershire sauce, balsamic vinegar, and water, and then sprinkle with onion soup mix and black pepper. Cover and cook on high for 4 hours. Allow to cool for 20 minutes, and then serve them on a large plate.

Nutrition: calories: 250 | fat: 6.0 g | protein: 33.0 g | carbs: 15.0 g | fiber: 3.0 g | sugar: 6.0 g | sodium: 510 mg

Tuna Teriyaki Kabobs

Prep time: 25 minutes | Serves 8

Ingredients:
1-1/2 lb tuna
2 red peppers medium sweet
1 sweet onion large
1/4 cup of fresh cilantro minced
1/4 cup of sesame oil
4 tbsp lime juice
3 tbsp soy sauce
3 tbsp olive oil extra virgin
1 tbsp fresh ginger root minced
2 minced garlic cloves
SALAD
1 package of baby spinach fresh

1 yellow pepper medium sweet
8 halved cherry tomatoes

Directions:
4 metal / moistened wooden skewers, threaded with tuna pieces 4 additional skewers should be pepper & onion slices. In a 13x9-inches of the baking dish, arrange the skewers. Combine marinade ingredients inside the mixing bowl. Half of the mix should be saved for the salad dressing. Pour the leftover marinade over the skewers and refrigerate for 30 mins. Cover & grill kabobs on moderate flame, flipping periodically, till tuna is just pink in the middle for about medium-rare (2-3 mins each side) and veggies become crisp-tender (2-3 mins per side) (10-12 mins). Remove your tuna kabobs from the grill & keep them warm while the veggies finish cooking. Toss the spinach, yellow pepper, & cherry tomatoes in the leftover dressing for the salad. Serve the tuna kabob & a veggie kabob on salad for every serving.

Nutrition: calories: 350 kcal | fats: 21 g | proteins: 17.7 g | carbohydrates: 47 g

Easy Lime Lamb Cutlets

Prep time: 4 hours 20 minutes | Cook time: 8 minutes | Serves 4

Ingredients:
¼ cup freshly squeezed lime juice
2 tbsp lime zest
2 tbsp chopped fresh parsley
Sea salt and freshly ground black pepper to taste
1 tbsp extra-virgin olive oil
12 lamb cutlets (about 1 ½lb/680 g in total)

Directions:
Combine the lime juice, zest, parsley, salt, black pepper, and olive oil in a large bowl. Stir to mix well. Dunk the lamb cutlets in the bowl of the lime mixture, and then toss to coat well. Wrap the bowl in plastic and refrigerate to marinate for at least 4 hours. Preheat the oven to 450°F (235°C) or broil. Line a baking sheet with aluminum foil. Remove the bowl from the refrigerator, let sit for 10 minutes, and discard the marinade. Arrange the lamb cutlets on the baking sheet.
Broil the lamb in the preheated oven for 8 minutes or until it reaches your desired doneness. Flip the cutlets with tongs to make sure they are cooked evenly.
Serve immediately.

Nutrition: calories: 297 | fat: 18.8 g | protein: 31.0 g | carbs: 1.0 g | fiber: 0 g | sugar: 0 g | sodium: 100 mg

Butter Sautéed Green Beans

Prep time: 15 minutes | Cook time: 5 minutes | Serves 4

Ingredients:
1 tbsp. butter
1 1/2 lbs. green beans, trimmed
1 tsp. ground nutmeg
Sea salt, to taste

Directions:
Melt the butter in a large skillet over medium heat. Sauté the green beans in the melted butter for 5 minutes until tender but still crisp, stirring. Season with nutmeg and salt and mix well. Remove from the heat and cool for a few minutes before serving.

Nutrition: calories: 82.6 | fat: 3g | protein: 3.7g | carbs: 11.8g | fiber: 6.1g | sugar: 2.8g

Sesame Chicken Stir Fry

Prep time: 10 minutes | Cook time: 30 minutes | Serves 2

Ingredients:
12 oz. Skinless, boneless chicken breast (340 gr)
1 tbsp. Vegetable oil
2 garlic cloves, finely minced
1 cup broccoli florets
1 cup cauliflowers
1/2 lb. fresh mushrooms, sliced (0,5/1kg)
4 green onions, cut into 1-inch pieces
2 tbsp. Low-sodium soy sauce
3 tbsp. Dry sherry
1 tsp. Finely minced fresh ginger
1/4 tsp. Sesame oil
1/4 cup dry-roasted peanuts
¼ cup arrowroot

Directions:
Cut off fat from chicken and thinly slice diagonally into 1-inch strips, Heat oil and stir-fry chicken in a vast non-stick skillet for 4 minutes. Remove; put aside and keep warm—Stir-fry garlic for 15 seconds; then broccoli and cauliflower, stir-fry for 2 minutes. Then fry mushrooms, green onions, soy sauce, sherry, and ginger for 2 minutes. Pour dissolved arrowroot, sesame oil, peanuts, and chicken. Cook until heated through and the sauce has thickened.

Nutrition: calories: 256g | carbohydrates: 9 g |fiber: 30 g

Sumptuous Lamb and Pomegranate Salad

Prep time: 8 hours 35 minutes | Cook time: 30 minutes | Serves 8

Ingredients:

1 ½cups pomegranate juice
4 tbsp olive oil, divided
1 tbsp ground cinnamon
1 tsp cumin
1 tbsp ground ginger
3 garlic cloves, chopped
Salt and freshly ground black pepper to taste
1 (4 lb/1.8 kg) lamb leg, deboned, butterflied, and fat trimmed 2 tbsp pomegranate balsamic vinegar
2 tsp Dijon mustard
½cup pomegranate seeds
5 cups of baby kale
4 cups fresh green beans, blanched
¼ cup toasted walnut halves
2 fennel bulbs, thinly sliced
2 tbsp Gorgonzola cheese

Directions:

Mix the pomegranate juice, 1 tbsp olive oil, cinnamon, cumin, ginger, garlic, salt, and black pepper in a large bowl. Stir to mix well. Dunk the lamb leg in the mixture and press to coat well. Wrap the bowl in plastic and refrigerate to marinate for at least 8 hours. Remove the bowl from the refrigerator and let sit for 20 minutes. Pat the lamb dry with paper towels. Preheat the grill to high heat.
Brush the grill grates with 1 tbsp olive oil, then arrange the lamb on the grill grates. Grill for 30 minutes. Remove the lamb from the grill and wrap it with aluminum foil. Let stand for 15 minutes.
Meanwhile, combine the vinegar, mustard, salt, black pepper, and remaining olive oil in a separate large bowl. Stir to mix well.
Add the remaining ingredients and lamb leg to the bowl and toss to combine well. Serve immediately.

Nutrition: calories: 380 | fat: 21.0 g | protein: 32.0 g | carbs: 16.0 g | fiber: 5.0 g | sugar: 6.0 g | sodium: 240 mg

Lemon chicken with peppers

Prep time: 5 minutes | Cook time: 20 minutes | Serves 3

Ingredients:

1 tsp. Cornstarch

1 tbsp. Low sodium soy sauce
12 oz. Chicken breast tenders, cut in thirds
1/4 cup fresh lemon juice
1/4 cup low sodium soy sauce
1/4 cup fat-free chicken broth
1 tsp. Fresh ginger, minced
2 garlic cloves, minced
1 tbsp. Splenda
1 tsp. Cornstarch
1 tbsp. Vegetable oil
1/4 cup red bell pepper
1/4 cup green bell pepper

Directions:
Scourge 1 tsp. Cornstarch and 1 tbsp. Soy sauce. Add sliced chicken tenders. Chill to marinate for 10 minutes. Stir the lemon juice, 1/4 cup soy sauce, chicken broth, ginger, garlic, Splenda, and 1 tsp. Cornstarch together. Warm-up oil in a medium frying pan. Cook chicken over medium-high heat for 4 minutes. Add sauce and sliced peppers. Cook 1 to 2 minutes more.
Nutrition: calories: 15g | carbohydrates: 6 g |fiber: 1 g

Pork Fillet on Lentils

Prep time: 10 minutes | Cook time: 25 minutes | Serves 2

Ingredients:
7 oz pork tenderloin (200gr)
3 oz red lentils (85gr)
2 onions
4 tsp oil
Curry
4 spring onions
1 apple

Directions:
Wash the pork tenderloin, pat dry, and cut into small medallions. Peel and dice the onions. Wash the leek and cut it into small rings. Peel the apple, remove the core and cut it into wedges. Fry the onions, leeks, and apple wedges in a pan with hot oil. Add the curry and the lentils. Punch with 100 ml of water. Put on the lid and simmer for 12 minutes. Add salt and pepper.
Fry the medallions vigorously in a second pan with hot oil (3 minutes on each side). Add salt and pepper. Serve the meat with lentil vegetables.

Nutrition: calories: 275 | fat: 7.0 g | protein: 23.0 g | carbs: 29.0 g | fiber: 4.0 g | sugar: 3.0 g | sodium: 250 mg

Orange Chicken in a Creamy Sauce

Ready in about 6 hours and 10 minutes | Serving 8 | Difficulty: hard

Ingredients:
3 tbsp of oil
4 lb. of skinless and bone-in chicken thighs (2kg)
1/2 cup of lemon juice
1/2 cup of vinegar (white wine)
1 tsp of orange zest, grated
3 tbsp of brandy
1/4 tsp of liquid stevia sweetener (lemon drop)
1/2 tsp of orange extract
6 oz. of cream cheese (170 gr)
8 sliced scallions
Black pepper, ground, to taste
Salt, to taste

Directions:
Brown the chicken in the oil in a large, heavy skillet set over medium heat. Transfer to a slow cooker and simmer on low for several hours. Pour the ingredients into a mixing bowl and stir well. Add the stevia and stir until it dissolves (about 30 seconds). Pour the sauce over the chicken—Cook for six hours on low with the lid on the pot. When the cooking time is complete, remove the chicken from the pan and place it on a plate. Cook for another minute or two after adding the scallions and cream cheese, constantly stirring until the cream cheese is completely melted. Season it with salt and freshly ground pepper. Serve the chicken with the sauce on the side.

Nutrition: kcal 384c fat: 24g | carbs: 4 g | protein: 34g

Turkey Rolls

Prep time: 8 hours 35 minutes | Cook time: 40 minutes | Serves 2

Ingredients:
2 turkey schnitzel (100 g each)
14 oz leek (396 gr)
2 oz long-grain rice (56 gr)
2 slices of salmon ham
2 oz Gouda (1 slice) (56 gr)
250 ml vegetable stock

Directions:

Wash the leek and cut off the ends. Put 4 leaves aside and blanch for 4
minutes. Cut the remaining leek into rings. Prepare the vegetable stock. Wash the turkey schnitzel, pat dry, and then place on the leek leaves. Halve the cheese slices and place a piece of cheese and a salmon ham on top of the turkey. Roll up the turkey escalope, pinch it with a wooden skewer and fry it in a pan with hot oil. Pour the curry over the skewers. Deglaze with the broth.
Put on the lid and let simmer for ¼ hour. Soak rice in salted boiling water for 20 minutes. Steam the leek in a pan with hot oil. Serve the rice with the leek and turkey rolls.

Nutrition: calories: 200 | fat: 8.0 g | protein: 30.0 g | carbs: 1.0 g | fiber: 0 g | sugar: 1.0 g | sodium: 394 mg

Baked Coconut Chicken Tenders

Prep Time: 10 minutes | Cooking Time: 20 minutes | Servings: 6

Ingredients:
4 chicken breasts each cut lengthwise into 3 strips 1/2 teaspoon salt
1/4 teaspoon freshly ground black pepper
1/2 cup coconut flour
2 eggs, beaten
2 tablespoons unsweetened plain almond milk
1 cup unsweetened coconut flakes

Directions:
Preheat the oven to 400 ºF (205 ºC). Line a baking sheet with parchment paper.
Season the chicken pieces with the salt and pepper.
Place the coconut flour in a small bowl. In another bowl, mix the eggs with the almond milk. Spread the coconut flakes on a plate.
One by one, roll the chicken pieces in the flour, then dip the floured chicken in the egg mixture and shake off any excess. Roll in the coconut flakes and transfer to the prepared baking sheet.
Bake for 15 to 20 minutes, flipping once halfway through, until cooked through and browned.

Nutrition: Calories: 216 | Fats: 13g | Proteins: 20g | Carbohydrates: 9g | Fibers: 6g | Sugars: 2g | Sodium: 346mg

Golden Triangle Kabobs

Ready in about 1 day and 2 hours | Serving 4 | Difficulty: Hard

Ingredients:
1 1/2 lb. of skinless and boneless chicken thighs (750 gr)
2 tbsp of lemon juice
1 tbsp of lime juice
1 minced shallot
5 crushed cloves of garlic
1 tbsp of grated ginger root
2 tbsp of soy sauce

3 drops of sweetener (liquid stevia)
1 tsp of ground turmeric

Directions:
Make 1-inch (2.5-cm) cubes of your chicken breasts. It's simpler to do this if the water is slightly frozen. In a large resealable plastic bag, place the chicken cubes, mix the rest of the ingredients and pour them over them. As you seal the bag, push out any remaining air as you go. Place the bag in the refrigerator for at least a few hours before using it. Consider soaking your bamboo skewers in the water if you're utilizing them later; when it comes time to cook supper, preheat your broiler or light your grill. Exit your refrigerator with the marinade in a small dish and set it aside for later use. Using 4 skewers, thread the chicken cubes onto the skewers. Begin grilling or broiling your skewers after soaking them in water for 5 minutes. Baste the kabobs on both sides with the leftover marinade (discard the remaining marinade to prevent the spread of germs), flip them over and cook for an additional 5 minutes, or until done.

Nutritional: kcal 210 | fat: 3g | carbs: 3g | protein: 40g

Garlic Cheese and Artichoke Stuffed Chicken Breasts

Ready in about 30 minutes | Serving 4 | Difficulty: Easy

Ingredients:
1 jar of marinated and drained artichoke hearts
1 1/2 lb. of skinless and boneless chicken breasts, 4 pieces (750 gr)
1/4 tsp of black pepper, ground
3 oz. of 1/2 tbsp of butter

Directions:
Preheat the oven to 375 °F (190 °C). Placing the chicken breasts one at a time in a large, heavy-duty resealable plastic bag and sealing it while pushing out any air helps the bag stay moist. Pound the chicken with whatever heavy object you have on hand until the meat is a quarter-inch (6 mm) thick over the whole surface. Repeat the process with the rest of the chicken breasts. Drain artichoke hearts and put them in a food processor fitted with an S-blade. Add cheese and process until smooth. Don't forget to add pepper. The artichokes should be finely diced but not puréed after pulsing them several times. Roll up jelly-roll style after spreading each breast with a fourth of the cheese mixture. Use toothpicks to keep the top closed. Turn the heat up to medium-high and coat the inside of a big, heavy pan with nonstick spray. The butter should be heated and swung around the pan to coat the bottom. Toss in the chicken rolls and cook for approximately 3 minutes on each side, or until they're gently golden brown. If the handle of your skillet isn't oven-safe, cover it with aluminum foil. Place everything in the oven for 15 minutes or until done.
Nutrition: kcal 298 | fat: 12g | carbs: 4g | protein: 41g

Eggplant and Bulgur Pilaf

Prep time: 10 minutes | Cook time: 60 minutes | Serves 4

Ingredients:
1 tbsp. extra-virgin olive oil
1/2 sweet onion, chopped
2 tsp. garlic, minced
1 cup eggplant, chopped
1 1/2 cups bulgur
4 cups low-sodium chicken broth
1 cup tomato, diced
Salt and freshly ground black pepper, to taste 2 tbsp. fresh basil, chopped

Directions:
Place a large saucepan over medium-high heat. Add the oil and sauté the onion and garlic until softened and translucent, about 3 minutes. Stir in the eggplant and sauté for 4 minutes to soften. Stir in the broth, bulgur, and tomatoes. Bring the mixture to a boil. Reduce the heat to low, cover, and simmer until the water has been absorbed about 50 minutes. Season the pilaf with salt and pepper. Garnish with the basil and serve.

Nutrition: calories: 299.8 | fat: 3.8g | protein: 14.7g | carbs: 53.7g | fiber: 12g | sugar: 6.7g

Butternut Curried Squash Soup

Ready in about 60 minutes | Servings 2 | Difficulty: Hard

Ingredients:
1 tbsp. of butter, 1 cup of chopped onions
1 tsp of curry powder
1 tsp of ground cinnamon
1/2 tsp of ground nutmeg
1/4 tsp of cayenne pepper, ground
3 pounds of peeled butternut squash (1,3 kgs)
2 cans of 14.5-oz. of chicken broth
2 cups of water
3 tsp of grated ginger
1 tsp of salt
1/4 tsp of pepper, ground
1/3 cup of heavy cream

Directions:
Melt some butter into a deep pot for soup and set to medium heat. Then, add some onions and cook until brown for 7 to 8 minutes. Mix some nutmeg, cinnamon, cayenne pepper, and curry powder, then cook it for 1 minute, until sweet-scented. Add squash, broth, ginger, water, pepper, and Salt. Raise the temperature to be high, then boil, then decrease the temperature and for 20 minutes, simmer until your squash is gentle. Remove the squash and puree it in sets; transfer it back to the pot. Boil gently for about 20 minutes, then add more fluid to thin your soup. Before serving it, stir in heavy cream and top with bacon (crispy cooked), Parmesan, scallions, and sour cream. Then, serve it with salad.

Nutrition: kcal 312 | fat: 11 g | carbs: 48.8 g | protein: 5.1 g

Noodles and Creamy Chicken in Bowl

Ready in about 5 minutes | Serving 1 | Difficulty: Easy

Ingredients:
1/4 cup of roasted and jarred red peppers
1 package of tofu shirataki
1 scallion 5 olives (Kalamata)
3 tbsp of cream cheese (chive-and-onion)
1 tbsp of minced parsley
Salt to taste
3 oz. of strips of chicken breast, precooked (85 gr)
Black grounded pepper, to taste

Directions:
Toss in the shirataki after draining and rinsing, then pop them in a microwave-safe bowl and cook for a couple of minutes. Cook them for 2 minutes on high for best results. Remove the roasted red peppers from the oven and drain well before dicing. Drain the shirataki one more when the microwave beeps. Add additional 2 minutes of cooking time to the pots. Make a pit out of your kalamatas and cut them up afterward. Similarly, slice your onion, reserving some crisp green portions for garnish, and cut your parsley. Drain your noodles for the last time and set them aside. Cook for another 30 seconds after adding the cream cheese, chicken breast strips, Salt, and pepper. Immediately after it comes out, add the olives, scallions, peppers, and parsley and mix well. Season it with Salt and pepper until the cheese has melted completely.

Nutrition: kcal 285 | fat: 22g | carbs: 5g | protein: 16g

Stir-fried steak and cabbage

Prep time: 15 minutes | Cook time: 10 minutes | Serves 4

Ingredients:
1/2 lb. sirloin steak, cut into strips (250 gr)

2 tsp—cornstarch
1-tbsp. Peanut oil
2 cups chopped red or green cabbage
1 yellow bell pepper, chopped
2 green onions, chopped
2 garlic cloves, sliced
1/2 cup commercial stir-fry sauce

Directions:
Toss the steak with the cornstarch and set it aside. In a 6-inch metal bowl, combine the peanut oil with the cabbage. Place in the basket and cook for 3 to 4 minutes. Remove the bowl from the basket and add the steak, pepper, onions, and garlic. Return to the air fryer and cook for 3 to 5 minutes. Add the stir-fry sauce and cook for 2 to 4 minutes. Serve over rice.

Nutrition: calories: 180 | carbohydrates: 9 g | fiber: 2 g

White Bean and Chicken Soup

Ready in about 25 minutes | Servings: 2 | Difficulty: Easy

Ingredients:
2 leeks, light green and white parts only, which are cut into quarter-inch rounds
2 tsp. Olive oil 1 roasted 2-pound chicken, discarded skin, removed meat from the bones, shredded 1 tbsp. fresh sage, chopped
2 cups of water
2 cans of less sodium in chicken broth
1 can of 15-ounce rinsed cannellini bean
Directions:
Heat the oil into your Dutch oven at a medium to high temperature. Add in some leeks and then cook, stir until soft for about three minutes. Mix in your sage and continue to cook until it becomes aromatic for about half min. Mix in the broth and some water and increase the temperature to high, then cover, and bring it to a boil. Put in some chicken and beans, cook uncovered, and occasionally stir until heated for about three minutes. Serve it hot.ù

Nutrition: kcal 276 | fat: 5.8g | carbs: 14.8g | protein: 35.1g

Roasted Tomato Brussels Sprouts

Prep Time: 15 minutes | Cooking Time: 20 minutes | Servings: 4
Ingredients:
1-pound (454 g) Brussels sprouts, trimmed and halved ½ cup sun-dried tomatoes, chopped
2 tablespoons freshly squeezed lemon juice
1 teaspoon lemon zest
From the Cupboard:

1 tablespoon extra-virgin olive oil
Sea salt and freshly ground black pepper, to taste.

Directions:
Preheat the oven to 400ºF (205ºC). Line a large baking sheet with aluminum foil.
Toss the Brussels sprouts in the olive oil in a large bowl until well coated. Sprinkle with salt and pepper.
Spread out the seasoned Brussels sprouts on the prepared baking sheet in a single layer.
Roast in the preheated oven for 20 minutes, shaking the pan halfway through, or until the Brussels sprouts are crispy and browned on the outside.
Remove from the oven to a serving bowl. Add the tomatoes, lemon juice, and lemon zest, and stir to incorporate. Serve immediately.

Nutrition: calories: 111 | fats: 5.8g | protein: 5.0g | carbs: 13.7g | fiber: 4.9g | sugar: 2.7g | sodium: 103mg

DINNER

Oven-Baked Potatoes and Green Beans

Prep time: 20 minutes | Cook time: 30 minutes | Serves 4

Ingredients:
1/2 lb. green beans (250 gr)
1/2 lb. potatoes, peeled and sliced into chunks (250 gr)
2 tsp. extra-virgin olive oil
1/2 tsp. garlic powder
2 tsp. Dijon mustard
Sea salt along with fresh ground black pepper as needed.

Directions:
Preheat the oven to 375°F (190°). Mix your chunks of potatoes with oil and mustard. Spread prepared potato chunks over a baking sheet. Bake for 15 minutes to make the first layer. Add your green beans, garlic powder, sea salt, and black pepper to your potatoes and toss—Bake for an additional 15 minutes. Serve and enjoy!

Nutrition: calories: 35 | carbohydrates: 5.5 g | protein: 1.3 g | fat: 0.3 g

Pork Chops and Butternut Squash Salad

Prep time: 20 minutes | Cook time: 25 minutes | Serves 4

Ingredients:
4 boneless pork chops
1 1/2 tbsp. fresh lemon juice
1 package of pomegranate seeds
1 package baby arugula
3 cups butternut squash, peeled and cubed
1/2 cup pine nuts
2 tbsp. extra-virgin olive oil (divided)
2 garlic cloves, minced
6 tbsp. balsamic vinaigrette
Sea salt along with fresh ground black pepper as needed

Directions:
Preheat your oven to 475°F(246°). Combine a tbsp: olive oil, minced garlic, and lemon juice. Mix your pork chops with an oil mixture and sprinkle the top of the chops with sea salt and pepper: Mix squash

and 1 tbsp. Oil, sprinkle with salt and pepper. Place your pork chops onto a baking sheet and add cubed squash around the chops. Bake for 25 minutes, then turn chops. Toast your pine nuts for about 5 minutes in a small pan over medium-high heat. Combine your squash, pine nuts, arugula, and pomegranate seeds. Drizzle with balsamic vinaigrette and toss. Serve and enjoy!

Nutrition: calories: 310 | carbohydrates: 2 g | protein: 20 g | fat: 17 g

Hummus and Salad Pita Flats

Prep time: 15 minutes | Cook time: 0 minutes | Serves 2

Ingredients:
2 oz. whole-wheat pitas
8 black olives, pitted
1/4 cup sweet roasted red pepper hummus
2 large eggs
2 tsp. spring mix
1 tsp. dried oregano
2 tsp. extra-virgin olive oil

Directions:
Heat your pitas according to the package instructions. Spread the hummus over the pitas—top pitas with hard-boiled eggs, dried oregano, and olives. Add the spring mix and extra-virgin olive oil. Serve and enjoy!

Nutrition: calories: 250 | carbohydrates: 50 g | protein: 8 g | fat: 2 g

Chicken Cordon Bleu

Prep time: 20 minutes | Cook time: 25 minutes | Serves 4

Ingredients:
8 chicken breasts, boneless and skinless
1/2 cup fat-free sour cream
2/3 cup skim milk
1 1/2 cups mozzarella cheese, grated
8 slices of ham
1 cup corn flakes, crushed
1 can low-fat condensed cream of chicken soup
1 tsp. lemon juice
1 tsp. paprika
1/2 tsp. garlic powder
1/2 tsp. black pepper

1/4 tsp. sea salt
Non-stick cooking spray as needed

Directions:
Heat your oven to 350°F(176°C). Spray a 13×9 baking dish lightly with cooking spray. Flatten the chicken breasts to 1/4-inch thick. Sprinkle with pepper and top with a slice of ham and 3 tbsp—cheese down the middle. Roll up, and tuck ends under and secure with toothpicks. Pour the milk into a shallow bowl. In another bowl, combine corn flakes and seasoning. Dip the chicken into milk, roll in the cornflake mixture, and then place on a prepared baking dish. Bake for 30 minutes or until your chicken is cooked through. Whisk the soup, lemon juice, and sour cream in a small pan until well combined. Cook over medium heat until hot. Remove the toothpicks from your chicken and place them onto serving plates. Top with sauce, serve and enjoy!

Nutrition: calories: 382 | carbohydrates: 9 g | protein: 50 g | fat: 14 g

Chicken Chili with Black Beans

Ready in about 30 minutes | Servings: 2 | Difficulty: Moderate

Ingredients:
1 and 3/4 pounds of cubed chicken breasts, skinless boneless 2 medium-sized chopped red peppers,
1 big chopped onion
3 tbsp. of olive oil
1 can of green chilies, chopped
4 minced garlic cloves
2 tbsp. of chili powder
2 tsp. of ground cumin
1 tsp. of ground coriander
2 cans of drained and rinsed black beans
1 can of Italian tomatoes, stewed
1 cup of beer or chicken broth
½-1 cup of water

Directions:
Cook the red peppers, onion, and chicken, in oil in your Dutch oven till the color of the chicken is not pink, approximately 5mins. Cook for 1 min more after adding the garlic, green chilies, garlic, cumin, chili powder, and coriander. Bring it to boil with the tomatoes, beans, 1/2 cup water, and broth. Reduce heat to low and cook for 15 minutes, stirring frequently, and add water as needed.

Nutrition: kcal 264 | fat: 6g | carbs: 21g | protein: 22g

Split English Pub Soup

Ready in about 20 minutes | Servings: 2 | Difficulty: Easy)

Ingredients:

2 chopped celery ribs
1 and a half cups of green peas, dried and split 1 big chopped carrot
4 cups of water
1 sweet chopped onion
1 bottle of light beer
1/2 cup of 2% milk
1 tbsp. of English mustard, prepared
1/4 cup of fresh parsley, minced
1 ham bone, meaty
1/4 tsp. of pepper
1/2 tsp. of salt
1/4 tsp. of ground nutmeg

Directions:

In a 4-quart slow cooker, place the ham bone. Peas, carrots, celery, and onion should be added at this point. Combine the beer, water, and mustard in a mixing bowl; pour over the veggies. Cook for 5-6 hrs. On high flame, covered, or till peas are cooked. Take the ham bone out of the soup. Allow to cool somewhat before trimming the fat and removing the flesh from the bone; discard the bones and fat. Put the meat in the slow cooker and chop it into bite-sized chunks. Combine the rest of the ingredients into a mixing bowl. Add more crushed parsley on top.

Nutritional: kcal 216 | fat: 1g | carbs: 25g | protein: 9g

Pesto Mayonnaise with Salmon

Ready in about 20 minutes | Serving 4 | Difficulty: Easy

Ingredients:

1/4 cup of mayonnaise
1 1/2 lb. of salmon fillet, chopped into 4 pieces 4 tbsp of shredded Parmesan (750 gr)
4 tsp of pesto sauce

Directions:

Using nonstick cooking spray, coat a shallow baking sheet and place the salmon fillets in it skin-side down. Bake for 15 minutes. Use a low-temperature broiler and cook the salmon for 5 minutes at approximately 10 cm (4 inches). In the meanwhile, whisk together the pesto sauce and mayonnaise. Continue broiling for 5 minutes, then top with pesto mayonnaise and finish with the salmon. A generous amount of Parmesan cheese should be sprinkled over each dish before eating. Return the plate to the oven for 1 1/2 minutes more, or until the gentle browning of cheese.

Nutrition: kcal 342 | fat: 21g | carbs: 1g | protein: 37g

Stuffed Peppers

Prep time: 15 minutes | Cook time: 30 minutes | Serves 4

Ingredients:
1 onion, diced
2 lb. Ground steak (1kg)
4 green bell peppers, seeds removed and cut in half
Sea salt along with black ground pepper
1 tbsp. Worcestershire sauce
2 tsp. garlic, minced
4 slices of mozzarella cheese
2 tbsp. oil

Directions:
Heat your oil, add diced onions, minced garlic, and salt and pepper in the pan over medium-high heat. Add chopped steak pieces into a Worcestershire saucepan and cook for 5 minutes. Add cooked steak and other ingredients into a bowl and combine (except cheese slices and pepper halves). Fill the pepper halves with a steak mixture and top with a thin piece of mozzarella cheese on top of each half pepper. Place the peppers into a baking pan and bake for 3o minutes. Serve and enjoy!

Nutrition: calories: 320 | carbohydrates: 10 g | protein: 40 g | fat: 19 g

Mediterranean Fish Fillets

Prep time: 10 minutes | Cook time: 3 minutes | Serves 4

Ingredients:
4 cod fillets
1 lb grape tomatoes, halved (450gr)
1 cup olives, pitted and sliced
2 tbsp capers
1 tsp dried thyme
2 tbsp olive oil
1 tsp garlic, minced
Pepper
Salt

Directions:
Pour 1 cup of water into the Instant Pot, then place the steamer rack in the pot. Spray heat-safe baking dish with cooking spray. Add half grape tomatoes into the dish and season with pepper and salt.

Arrange fish fillets on top of cherry tomatoes. Drizzle with oil and season with garlic, thyme, capers, pepper, and salt. Spread olives and remaining grape tomatoes on top of fish fillets. Place dish on top of steamer rack in the pot. Seal the pot with a lid, select manual, and cook on high for 3 minutes. Once done, release pressure using quick release. Remove lid. Serve and enjoy.

Nutrition: calories: 212 | fat: 11.9 g | carbs: 7.1 g | sugar: 3 g | protein: 21.4 g | cholesterol: 55 mg

Tuna Carbonara

Prep time: 5 minutes | Cook time: 25 minutes | Serves 4

Ingredients:
½lb tuna fillet, cut into pieces (226 gr)
2 eggs
4 tbsp fresh parsley, diced
From the store cupboard:
½homemade pasta, cook and drain
½cup reduced-fat Parmesan cheese
2 garlic cloves, peeled
2 tbsp extra-virgin olive oil
Salt and pepper to taste

Directions:
In a small bowl, beat the eggs, Parmesan, and a dash of pepper. Heat the oil in a large skillet over med-high heat. Add garlic and cook until browned. Add the tuna and cook for 2–3 minutes, or until the tuna is almost cooked through. Discard the garlic. Add the pasta and reduce the heat. Stir in egg mixture and cook for about 2 minutes, constantly stirring. If the sauce is too thick, thin with water, a little bit at a time until it has a creamy texture. Salt and pepper to taste and serve garnished with parsley.

Nutrition: calories: 409 | total carbs: 7 g | net carbs: 6 | protein: 25 g | fat: 30 g | sugar: 3 g | fiber: 1 g

Cajun Beef and Rice Skillet

Prep time: 10 minutes | Cook time: 25 minutes | Serves 4

Ingredients:
2 cups cauliflower rice, cooked
3/4 lb. lean ground beef
1 red bell pepper, sliced thin
1 jalapeno pepper, with seeds removed and diced fine
1 celery stalk, sliced thin
1/2 yellow onion, diced
1/4 cup parsley, fresh diced
4 tsp. Cajun seasoning

1/2 cup low-sodium beef broth

Directions:
Place the beef with 1 1/2 tsp—Cajun seasoning into a large skillet over medium-high heat. Add the vegetables, except cauliflower and remaining Cajun seasoning. Cook, occasionally stirring, for about 8 minutes or until vegetables are tender. Add the broth, stir, and cook for 3 minutes or until the mixture thickens. Stir in your cauliflower rice and cook until heated through.
Remove from heat and add to serving bowls, then top with parsley, serve and enjoy!

Nutrition: calories: 198 | carbohydrates: 8 g | protein: 28 g | fat: 6 g

Bone Broth

Prep time: 10 minutes | Cook time: 25 minutes | Serves 4

Ingredients:
1 chicken carcass and dripping or 1 large marrow bone 1 chopped onion
1 stalk of chopped celery
1tbsp. minced garlic
1tbsp. bouillon powder
2 cups water

Directions:
Place the chicken, onion, and celery in your Instant Pot. Cover with 2 cups of water. Seal and cook on Manual, high pressure, for 60 minutes. Release the pressure naturally. Strain the solids out. Add the garlic and bouillon.

Nutrition: calories: 38 | carbohydrates: 2 g | protein: 3 g | fat: 2 g | sugar: 0 g

Tofu Mushrooms

Prep time: 5 minutes | Cook time: 10 minutes | Serves 3

Ingredients:
1 block tofu
1 cup mushrooms
4 tbsp. butter
4 tbsp. parmesan cheese
Salt to taste
Ground black pepper to taste

Directions:

Toss tofu cubes with melted butter, salt, and black pepper in a mixing bowl. Sauté the tofu within 5 minutes. Stir in cheese and mushrooms. Sauté for another 5 minutes.

Nutrition: calories: 211 | carbohydrates: 2 g | protein: 11.5 g | fat: 18.5 g | cholesterol: 51 mg | sodium: 346 mg

Spinach Rich Ballet

Prep time: 5 minutes | Cook time: 30 minutes | Serves 4

Ingredients:
1 1/2 lbs. baby spinach
8 tsp. coconut cream
14 oz. cauliflower
2 tbsp. unsalted butter
Salt to taste
Ground black pepper to taste

Directions:
Warm-up oven at 360°F (182°C). Melt butter, then toss in spinach to sauté for 3 minutes. Divide the spinach into four ramekins. Divide cream, cauliflower, salt, and black pepper in the ramekins. Bake within 25 minutes.

Nutrition: calories: 188 | protein: 14.6 g | fat: 12.5 g | cholesterol: 53 mg | sodium: 1098 mg

Cheesy Beef and Noodles

Prep time: 10 minutes | Cook time: 15 minutes | Serves 4

Ingredients:
1 lb. lean ground beef (450 gr)
2 cups mozzarella cheese, grated
1 onion, diced
1/2 cup + 2 tbsp. fresh parsley, diced
1 package of Fettuccine noodles
2 tbsp. tomato paste
1 tbsp. Worcestershire sauce
1 tbsp. extra-virgin olive oil
3 garlic cloves, minced
1 tsp. red pepper flakes
Sea salt and black pepper to taste
1/2 cup water

Directions:

Heat your oil in a large skillet placed over medium-high heat. Add the beef and cook while breaking up with the spatula for about 2 minutes. Cook the noodles according to package instructions. Lower the heat of your skillet to medium, then season with salt an pepper. Stir in your garlic, pepper flakes, onion, tomato paste, 1/2 cup parsley, Worcestershire sauce, and 1/2 cup water. Bring to a simmer while occasionally stirring for about 8 minutes. Stir in the cooked noodles and continue to cook for another 2 minutes. Stir 1 cup of cheese over the top and cover with a lid until cheese melts. Serve garnishing with remaining parsley and enjoy!

Nutrition: calories: 372 | carbohydrates: 7 g | protein: 44 g | fat: 18 g

Red Clam Sauce and Pasta

Prep time: 10 minutes | Cook time: 3 hours | Serves 4

Ingredients:
1 onion, diced
¼ cup fresh parsley, diced
From the store cupboard:
2 (6 ½oz) cans of clams, chopped, undrained
14 ½oz tomatoes, diced, undrained
6 oz tomato paste
2 garlic cloves, diced
1 bay leaf
1 tbsp sunflower oil
1 tsp Splenda
1 tsp basil
½tsp thyme
½homemade pasta, cook and drain

Directions:
Heat oil in a small skillet over med-high heat. Add onion and cook until tender; add garlic and cook 1 minute more. Transfer to the crockpot. Add remaining ingredients, except pasta, cover, and cook on low for 3–4 hours. Discard bay leaf and serve over cooked pasta.

Nutrition: calories: 223 | total carbs: 32 g | net carbs: 27 g | protein: 12 g | fat: 6 g | sugar: 15 g | fiber: 5 g

Roasted Turkey with Cranberries And Peaches

Ready in about 7 hours | Serving 8 | Difficulty: Hard

Ingredients:
2 tbsp of olive oil

3 lb. of turkey roast (1,35 kg)
1/2 cup of chopped onion
1 cup of cranberries
3 tbsp of spicy mustard
1/4 cup of sweetener (erythritol)
1 chopped and peeled peach
1/4 tsp of flakes of red pepper

Directions:
Your turkey roast will likely be similar to mine (a Butterball), a boneless affair consisting of light and dark flesh wrapped into an oval roast and sealed in a net bag. Allow it to cook in the net to avoid it falling apart on you. Heat oil in a large, heavy pan over medium-high heat, and roast the turkey until brown on both sides. Place it in a slow cooker on low heat. Then, in the bowl of your food processor fitted with the S-blade, combine the cranberries, red onion, erythritol, mustard, and red pepper flakes. Puree the mixture until it has a gritty texture to it. Pour this sauce over the roast beef. Set the slow cooker on low, cover it, and let it do its thing for 6 to 8 hours. Place the roast on a serving dish and toss with the sauce. To serve the sauce with the turkey, transfer it to a sauce boat. You may remove the netting before filling the turkey if you like, but I find it simpler to use a nice sharp knife to slice straight through the net and let each diner take their piece.

Nutrition: kcal 255 | fat: 8g | carbs: 4g | protein: 31g

Gingered Monkfish

Ready in about 15 minutes | Serving 4 | Difficulty: Easy

Ingredients:
1 tbsp of grated ginger root
1 ib. of monkfish
2 tsp of paste of chili garlic
1 tbsp of Ketchup, Reduced Sugar
3 scallions
6 oz. of asparagus
1 tsp of sesame oil (dark)
1 tbsp of peanut oil

Directions:
Remove the monkfish's membrane with a sharp knife, then cut it into thin, flat, circular slices. Reserve. In a small mixing bowl, combine the ketchup, ginger root, and chili garlic paste until well combined. Apply a thin layer of this mixture to the monkfish slices. Allow for 5 minutes of resting time. Wait until the asparagus is ready to be snapped at the ends where it naturally wants to break. On a diagonal cut, the spears to a length of 1 inch (2.5 cm). Slice your scallions as well, making sure to include the sharp green portion of the green. You may use your wok for this if you have one. If you don't have one, use a big, heavy skillet, but spray it with nonstick cooking spray beforehand. In any case, heat the pan over

high heat while adding the peanut oil. In a separate bowl, combine monkfish with its sauce, asparagus, and scallion until everything is well distributed. Stir-fry the fish very carefully so that it does not get mushy. The fish should be done and the veggies crisp-tender, approximately 5 minutes. Add the sesame oil and gently mix everything before serving.

Nutrition: kcal 139 | fat: 6g | carbs: 3g | protein: 17g

Shrimp and Artichoke Skillet

Prep time: 5 minutes | Cook time: 10 minutes | Serves 4

Ingredients:
1 ½cup shrimp, peel and devein
2 shallots, diced
1 tbsp margarine
From the store cupboard:
2 (12 oz) jars of artichoke hearts, drain and rinse 2 cups of white wine
2 garlic cloves, diced fine

Directions:
Melt margarine in a large skillet over med-high heat. Add shallot and garlic and cook until they start to brown, stirring frequently. Add artichokes and cook for 5 minutes. Reduce heat and add wine. Cook for 3 minutes, stirring occasionally. Add the shrimp and cook just until they turn pink. Serve.

Nutrition: calories: 487 | total carbs: 26 g | net carbs: 17 g | protein: 64 g | fat: 5 g | sugar: 3 g | fiber: 9 g

Lettuce Salad with Lemon

Prep time: 10 minutes | Cook time: 30 minutes | Serves 4

Ingredients:
2 oz. arugula
1/2 head Romaine lettuce, chopped
1 avocado, pitted and sliced
2 tsp. extra-virgin olive oil
1 tbsp. lemon juice
Sea salt along with fresh ground black pepper as needed

Directions:
Whisk your torn arugula, lemon juice, chopped avocado, olive oil, sea salt, and pepper. Add the chopped lettuce and toss to coat. Serve and enjoy!

Nutrition: calories: 15 | carbohydrates: 1 g | protein: 2 g | fat: 2 g

Dill and Poached Trout

Ready in about 15 minutes | Serving 2 | Difficulty: Easy

Ingredients:

1 tbsp of lemon juice
2 tbsp of white wine, dry
12 oz. of trout fillet
1 tbsp of dill weed, snipped
Black pepper, ground, to taste
Salt, to taste

Directions:

Combine the lemon juice and wine in a small, non-reactive pan with a tight-fitting cover. Place the pan over medium heat and bring it to a gentle simmer. Combine the dill with the wine–lemon juice combination and place the fish fillets skin side in the mixture. Reduce the heat to low and cover the pan with a lid; set the timer for eight minutes. Using two serving plates, carefully move the trout fillets and place them skin-side down on each plate throughout the transfer. Serve with the liquid from the pan and a little salt and pepper if you're feeling adventurous.

Nutrition: kcal 265 | fat: 11g | carbs: 1g | protein: 35g

Alaskan Crab Omelette

Prep time: 10 minutes | Cook time: 1 minutes | Serves 1

Ingredients:

¼ cup cooked Alaskan crab meat
2 snow peas, trimmed, thinly sliced diagonally
½ shallot, finely sliced
½ chili, thinly sliced at an angle
1 tsp soy sauce
A few drops of sesame oil
1 egg
1 tsp vegetable oil

Directions:

Start by tossing crab meat with snow peas, shallot, and chili in a small bowl. Whisk egg with soy sauce and a tsp cold water in another bowl. Stir in sesame oil and pepper, then mix well. Spray a non-stick skillet and place it over medium-high heat. Pour this egg mixture into the skillet and spread it into a thin layer. Cook for 30 seconds, then spread the crab mixture over the egg 7. Fold the egg omelet over the crab mixture. Serve warm.

Nutrition: calories: 317 | total fat: 31.1 g | saturated fat: 7.6 g | cholesterol: 77 mg | sodium: 112 mg | total carbs: 9.7 g | fiber: 0 g | sugar: 7.4 g | protein: 1.4 g

Salmon Milano

Prep time: 10 minutes | Cook time: 20 minutes | Serves 6

Ingredients:
2 ½lb salmon filet
2 tomatoes, sliced
½cup margarine
From the store cupboard:
½cup basil pesto

Directions:
Heat the oven to 400°F(200°C). Line a 9x15-inch baking sheet with foil, ensuring it covers the sides. Place another large piece of foil onto the baking sheet and place the salmon filet on top of it. Place the pesto and margarine in a blender or food processor and pulse until smooth. Spread evenly over salmon. Place tomato slices on top. Wrap the foil around the salmon, tenting around the top to prevent foil from touching the salmon as much as possible. Bake 15–25 minutes, or salmon flakes easily with a fork. Serve.

Nutrition: calories: 444 | total carbs: 2 g | protein: 55 g | fat: 24 g | sugar: 1 g | fiber: 0 g

Onion Tofu

Prep time: 8 minutes | Cook time: 5 minutes | Serves 3

Ingredients:
2 blocks of tofu
2 onions
2 tbsp. butter
1 cup cheddar cheese
Salt to taste
Ground black pepper to taste

Directions:
Rub the tofu with salt and pepper in a bowl. Add melted butter and onions to a skillet to sauté within 3 minutes. Toss in tofu and stir cook for 2 minutes. Stir in cheese and cover the skillet for 5 minutes on low heat. Serve.

Nutrition: Calories: 184 | Carbohydrates: 6.3 g | Protein: 12.2 g | Fat: 12.7 g | Sugar: 2.7 g | Fiber: 1.6 g

APPETIZERS

Taco Casserole

Prep time: 10 minutes | Cook time: 60 minutes

Ingredients:
1-pound lean ground pork
1 small cauliflower, chopped
1 whole jalapeno, chopped
¼ cup chopped green bell pepper
¼ cup chopped red onion
¼ cup chopped tomato
1 tsp. Cumin
1 tsp. Cilantro
Pinch of turmeric
1 tbsp. Minced garlic
1 cup pepper jack cheese, shredded
½ cup Monterey jack cheese, shredded
1 cup sour cream

Directions:
Preheat the oven to 350 degrees F(176°C).Place the minced pork and cauliflower in a bowl and add the spices and herbs. Add the onions, tomato, peppers and jalapeno. Mix in 1 cup of Monterey Jack cheese. Pour this into a casserole dish. Top with the remaining cheese. Bake for 1 hour. Top with sour cream.
Nutrition: Calories: 247 | Carbohydrates: 30.3 g | Protein: 18.2 g | Fat: 7 g | Sugar: 7 g

No-Carb Cheese Bread with Dry Salami

Prep time: 10 minutes | Cook time: 20 minutes

Ingredients:
1 ¼ cup Monterey jack cheese shredded
¼ cup coconut flour
3 tbsp. Flaxseed meal
1 extra-large egg
½ tsp. Italian seasoning
3 small slices of Italian dry salami
4 small pieces of provolone cheese

¾ ounce spinach leaves
¼ cup jalapeno sliced
2 tbsp. Extra virgin olive oil
1 extra-large egg yolk

Directions:
Pinch of sea salt. Preheat the oven to 400 degrees F(202°C). Mix the coconut flour, flaxseed meal and seasoning. In a mixing bowl, melt the pepper jack cheese in a microwave. Add one whole egg to the melted cheese and the dry coconut flour mix. Combine until well mixed. Spread out a piece of parchment paper and put the dough on top Top it off with another piece of parchment paper and use a rolling pin to flatten the dough into an oval disc. Layer with salami and cheese and torn spinach leaves. Layer with jalapeno and drizzle with olive oil. Season with sea salt. Cut into diagonal strips. Fold the ends of the dough. Braid the strips on top. Bake for 15 to 20 minutes until the braid is golden brown.
Nutrition: Calories: 380 | Carbohydrates: 44.3 g | Protein: 19 g | Fat: 17 g | Fiber: 4g

Low Carb Tortilla

Prep time: 10 minutes | Cook time: 15 minutes

Ingredients:
1 ¼ cup almond flour
2 teaspoons xanthan gum
1 teaspoon baking powder
1/4 teaspoon sea salt fine
2 teaspoons distilled vinegar
1 egg lightly beaten
3 teaspoons water

Directions:
Combine almond flour, xanthan gum, baking powder & salt n a food processor. Pour vinegar as the food processor is running. Pour in the egg and mix well. Pour the water and continue processing until it forms a dough. Wrap the dough in cling wrap and knead it with the plastic around it. Let it rest for 10 min. Over medium heat, sprinkle water until droplets evaporates. Divide into 8 dough balls and roll out between two sheets of parchment using a rolling pin. Cook over medium heat for 4 to 5 seconds per side before flipping. Please do this for the next 30 to 40 seconds and make sure you don't overcook them. Keep them warm and reheat when ready to use.

Nutrition: Calories: 80 | Carbohydrates: 13 g | Protein: 19 g | Fat: 0.7 g | Fiber: 3g

Low Carb Tortilla Chips

Prep time: 10 minutes | Cook time: 15 minutes

Ingredients:
6 ounces mozzarella, shredded
3 ounces almond flour
2 tbsp ricotta cheese
2 egg
Sea salt to taste
1/2 tsp cumin powder
1 tsp coriander/cilantro powder
A pinch of chili powder

Directions:
Preheat the 425 degrees F. Combine the shredded mozzarella and almond flour, and cheese. Microwave for 1 minute over high heat. Stir and microwave again for 30 seconds on the highest setting. Add the eggs, salt, coriander, cumin and chili powder. Place the pastry between 2 pcs. of parchment paper and flatten with a rolling pin. Slide in a pizza stone and bake for 13 min. or until browned. Take it out of the oven, cut it into triangles, and bake once more for 4 min.
Nutrition: Calories: 85 | Carbohydrates: 11 g | Protein: 19 g | Fat: 1.7 g | Fiber: 2.5g

10-hour Roasted Tomatoes

Prep time: 10 minutes | Cook time: 10 Hour

Ingredients:
30 ripe tomatoes, sliced in half crosswise.
¾ cup extra virgin olive oil
3 tbsp. Italian Seasoning
2 tbsp. Sea Salt
1/4 tsp. Black Pepper
2 tbsp. liquid stevia

Directions:
Preheat the oven to 170 degrees F(76°C). Place the tomatoes in a baking pan with the cut side up. Drizzle with 2/3 cup extra virgin olive oil, stevia, Italian seasoning, black pepper and salt. Bake for 10 hours. Drizzle with the remaining olive oil when you serve.
Cook's Note:
Do this overnight.
Nutrition: Calories: 57 | Carbohydrates: 14 g | Protein: 14 g | Fat: 0.17 g | Fiber: 2.7g

All-natural Bacon-wrapped Asparagus

Prep time: 10 minutes | Cook time: 15 minutes

Ingredients:
1 ½ lb. asparagus spears, trimmed 4 to 5 inches long tips Olive oil, for drizzling
A few pinches of assorted peppercorns
4 slices of natural nitrate-free bacon

Directions:
Preheat the oven to 400 degrees F(202°C). Lightly coat the asparagus spears in olive oil. Season with assorted peppercorns. Divide the spears and wrap them with bacon. Do this for all the asparagus spears and transfer to a greased cookie sheet. Bake for 12 min.
Nutrition: Calories: 167 | Carbohydrates: 3 g | Protein: 6 g | Fat: 17 g | Fiber: 1.7g

Crispy Kale Chips

Prep time: 10 minutes | Cook time: 25 minutes

Ingredients:
7 ounces Kale
1/4 cup olive oil
1/4 tsp. Sea salt
¼ tsp. cayenne pepper (optional)

Directions:
Pinch of black pepper. Preheat the oven to 300 degrees F (150 °C) and line 2 cookie sheets with parchment paper. Wash and dry the greens and tear the leaves into ½ inch strips. Lay them on a single layer and spray with peanut oil. Sprinkle with salt. Sprinkle with cayenne pepper and black pepper. Bake for 20 min. Until dry and darkened. Remove from the heat.
Note:
This makes for a perfect healthy snack and can be made up to 2 days ahead.

Nutrition: Calories: 140 | Carbohydrates: 7 g | Protein: 7 g | Fat: 10 g | Fiber: 3g

Starch-free Fried Calamari

Prep time: 10 minutes | Cook time: 5 minutes

Ingredients:
3 to 4 cups vegetable oil
One lb. squid washed and cut into 1/2-inch rings 2 cups almond flour
1 tablespoon cayenne pepper

Kosher salt
Lemon wedges, for garnish

Directions:
Preheat the oven to 200 degrees F(93°C). Add oil to the pan and heat over medium. Combine the almond flour and cayenne pepper and toss ½ of the calamari in the almond flour mixture. Tap to shake off the excess flour. Fry in hot oil until pale gold. Make sure not to overcrowd the pan. Season with salt. Drain on paper towels. Warm them in the oven.

Nutrition: Calories: 125 | Carbohydrates: 7 g | Protein: 8 g | Fat: 12g | Fiber: 2g

DESSERTS

Berry Sorbet

Prep time: 10 minutes | Cook time: 20 minutes | Serves 6

Ingredients:
2 cups water
2 cups blended strawberries
1 ½ tsp spelled flour
½ cup date sugar

Directions:
Add the water into a large pot and let the water begin to warm. Add the flour and date sugar and stir until dissolved. Allow this mixture to start boiling and cook for around ten minutes. It should have started to thicken. Please take off the heat and set it to the side to cool. Once the syrup has cooled off, add the strawberries, and stir well to combine. Pour into a container that is freezer safe and put it into the freezer until frozen. Take sorbet out of the freezer, cut it into chunks, and put it into a blender or food processor. Hit the pulse button until the mixture is creamy. Pour this into the same freezer-safe container and put it back into the freezer for four hours.

Nutrition: calories: 99 | carbs: 8 g

Shortbread Cookies

Prep time: 10 minutes | Cook time: 70 minutes | Serves 6

Ingredients:
2 ½cup almond flour
6 tbsp nut butter

½cup Erythritol
1 tsp vanilla essence

Directions:
Preheat your oven to 350°F(176°C). Layer a cookie sheet with parchment paper. Beat butter with Erythritol until fluffy. Stir in vanilla essence and almond flour. Mix well until it becomes crumbly. Spoon out a tbsp of cookie dough onto the cookie sheet. Add more dough to make as many cookies as possible. Bake for 15 minutes until brown.

Nutrition: calories: 288 | total fat: 25.3 g | saturated fat: 6.7 g | cholesterol: 23 mg | total carbs: 9.6 g sugar: 0.1 g | fiber: 3.8 g | sodium: 74 mg | potassium: 3 mg | protein: 7.6 g

Peanut Butter Bars

Prep time: 10 minutes | Cook time: 10 minutes | Serves 6

Ingredients:
¾ cup almond flour
2 oz almond butter
¼ cup swerve
½cup peanut butter
½tsp vanilla

Directions:
Combine all the ingredients for bars. Transfer this mixture to a 6-inch small pan. Press it firmly. Refrigerate for 30 minutes. Slice and serve.

Nutrition: calories: 214 | total fat: 19 g | saturated fat: 5.8 g | cholesterol: 15 mg | total carbs: 6.5 g sugar: 1.9 g | fiber: 2.1 g | sodium: 123 mg | protein: 6.5 g

Zucchini Bread Pancakes

Prep time: 15 minutes | Cook time: 35 minutes | Serves 3

Ingredients:
1 tbsp grapeseed oil
½ cup chopped walnuts
2 cups walnut milk
1 cup shredded zucchini
¼ cup mashed burro banana
2 tbsp date sugar
2 cups Kamut flour or spelled

Directions:
Place the date sugar and flour into a bowl. Whisk together. Add in the mashed banana and walnut milk. Stir until combined. Remember to scrape the bowl to get all the dry mixture. Add in walnuts and zucchini. Stir well until combined. Place the grapeseed oil onto a grill and warm. Pour 25 cups of batter on the hot griddle. Leave it along until bubbles begin forming on to surface. Carefully turn over the pancake and cook another four minutes until cooked through. Place the pancakes onto a serving plate and enjoy with some agave syrup.

Nutrition: calories: 246 | carbs: 49.2 g | fiber: 4.6 g | protein: 7.8 g

Coconut Chip Cookies

Prep time: 10 minutes | Cook time: 15 minutes | Serves 4

Ingredients:
1 cup almond flour
½ cup cacao nibs
½ cup coconut flakes, unsweetened
⅓cup Erythritol ½ cup almond butter
¼ cup nut butter, melted
¼ cup almond milk Stevia, to taste
¼ tsp sea salt

Directions:
Preheat your oven to 350°F(176°C). Layer a cookie sheet with parchment paper. Add and combine all the dry ingredients in a glass bowl. Whisk in butter, almond milk, vanilla essence, Stevia, and almond butter. Beat well, then stir in dry mixture. Mix well. Spoon out a tbsp cookie dough on the cookie sheet. Add more dough to make as many as 16 cookies. Flatten each cookie using your fingers. Bake for 25 minutes until golden brown. Let them sit for 15 minutes.

Nutrition: calories: 192 | total fat: 17.44 g | saturated fat: 11.5 g | cholesterol: 125 mg | total carbs: 2.2 g | sugar: 1.4 g | fiber: 2.1 g | sodium: 135 mg | protein: 4.7 g

Walnut Italian Cake

Ready in about 20 minutes | Serving 12 | Difficulty: Moderate

Ingredients:
1/2 cup of erythritol, divided
12 oz. of walnuts
cream of tartar, pinch
4 eggs

2 tsp of lemon zest
1/3 tsp of sweetener
2 tbsp of erythritol, powdered, for topping
Salt as needed

Directions:
Preheat the oven to 350 °F (180 °C). 9-inch springform pan coated with nonstick cooking spray, lined with baking paper or reusable nonstick pan liner. Place the walnuts in a food processor fitted with an S-blade and pulse until finely chopped. Pulse until the nuts are finely minced but not powdery. Process until the nuts are coarsely crushed but not greasy, with 2 tbsp (30 g) of erythritol added at a time. (Be careful not to overprocess.) (You don't want nut butter, do you? Prepare your eggs by separating them. To avoid the egg yolk from ruining your whites, divide them into tiny dishes or cups before adding the whites to your bowl. This will prevent the whites from refusing to whip when you add them! On the other hand, breaking a yolk simply messes up the white.

Nutrition: kcal 195 | fat: 18g | carbs: 4g | protein: 9g

Mixed Berries Cups

Ready in about 15 minutes | Serving 6 | Difficulty: Easy

Ingredients:
1 cup of boiling water
1 package of raspberry gelatin, sugar-free
zest of 1/2 orange, grated
2 tsp of lemon juice
1 cup of heavy cream
12 drops of vanilla-flavored sweetener
3/4 cups of thawed and frozen blackberries

Directions:
Place the water, gelatin, orange zest, and lemon juice in a blender and mix on high for 10 to 15 seconds, or until the gelatin is completely dissolved. Just long enough to incorporate the blackberries, add them back in, and whirl until well combined. Refrigerate the blender container for 10 minutes or until the mixture thickens. After adding the heavy cream (about 3/4 cup or 175 ml), pulse the blender to combine everything. Pour the mixture into 6 beautiful small dessert cups and place them in the refrigerator. Garnish each dish with 1/4 cup (60 ml) vanilla liquid stevia cream.

Nutrition: kcal 156 | fat: 15g | carbs: 5g | protein: 1g

Glazed Walnuts

Ready in about 2 hours and 20 min | Serving 6 | Difficulty: Hard)

Ingredients:
Boiling water
1 1/2 cups of walnuts
1 tbsp of erythritol
Coconut oil
1/2 tsp of vanilla extract

Directions:
Fill a basin halfway with boiling water and add the walnuts. Allow them to sit for no more than 4 or 5 minutes before draining thoroughly. Whisk together the vanilla and salt in a separate bowl until it is equally distributed. Using your hands, toss the vegetables until they are all similarly covered with erythritol. Allow an hour or two of drying time after spreading your walnuts on a dish. When you cook them, this will help to reduce spitting. Melt the coconut oil in a large, heavy pan over medium heat. Fry a handful of walnuts occasionally, stirring often, until golden and crisp. Allow cooling before storing in a jar with a tight-fitting cover.

Nutrition: kcal 191 | fat: 18g | carbs: 4g | protein: 8g

Cheesecake

Ready in about 2 hours | Serving 10 | Difficulty: Hard

Ingredients:
2 cups of Splenda
2 lb. of cream cheese
5 eggs
3 tbsp of heavy cream

Directions:
Preheat the oven to 375 °F (190 °C). Using an electric mixer, thoroughly combine all of the ingredients. Bake for 9 minutes in a greased 9-inch (23-centimeter) springform pan. 10 minutes in the oven should do the trick. Continue baking for an additional hour at a temperature of 250°F (120°C). Remove the cake from the oven and run a knife along the pan's edge. Return the cake to the hot oven and keep it there until the range is freezing (approximately another hour). Refrigerate overnight to allow flavors to blend.

Nutrition: kcal 365 | fat: 36g | carbs: 3g | protein: 10g

Creamy Cheese Balls

Ready in about 10 minutes | Serving 8 | Difficulty: Easy

Ingredients:
1 package of gelatin, sugar-free
8 oz. of chilled cream cheese

Directions:
Cut the cream cheese bar into 16 equal pieces using a sharp knife. Roll each one into a ball with your clean hands. Make gelatin balls by pouring the gelatin over a plate and rolling them in the powder until they are well coated. That's all there is to it. Keep them in an airtight jar in the refrigerator.

Nutrition: kcal 103 | fat: 10g | carbs: 1g | protein: 3g

Blackberry Soufflés

Prep time: 15 minutes | Cook time: 30 minutes | Serves 4

Ingredients:
12 oz. blackberries
4 egg whites
1/3 cup Splenda
1 tbsp. water
1 tbsp. Swerve powdered sugar
Nonstick cooking spray

Directions:
Heat oven to 375°F(190°C). Spray 4 1 cup ramekins with cooking spray. In a small saucepan, over med-high heat, combine blackberries and 1tbsp. Water, bring to a boil. Reduce heat and simmer until berries are soft. Add Splenda and stir over medium heat until Splenda dissolves, without boiling. Bring back to boiling, reduce heat and simmer for 5 minutes. Remove from heat and cool for 5 minutes. Place a fine-meshed sieve over a small bowl and push the berry mixture through it using the back of a spoon. Discard the seeds. Cover and chill for 15 minutes. In a large bowl, beat egg whites until soft peaks form. Gently fold in berry mixture. Spoon evenly into prepared ramekins and place them on a baking sheet. Bake 12 minutes, or until puffed and light brown. Dust with powdered Swerve and serve immediately.

Nutrition: calories: 141 | carbohydrates: 26 g | net carbohydrates: 21 g | protein: 5 g | fat: 0 g | sugar: 20 g | fiber: 5 g

Apricot Soufflé

Prep time: 5 minutes | Cook time: 30 minutes | Serves 4

Ingredients:
4 egg whites
3 egg yolks, beaten
3 tbsp. margarine
3/4 cup sugar-free apricot fruit spread
1/3 cup dried apricots, diced fine
1/4 cup warm water
2 tbsp. flour
1/4 tsp. cream of tartar
1/8 tsp. salt

Directions:
Heat oven to 325°F(162°C).
In a medium saucepan, over medium heat, melt margarine. Stir in flour and cook, stirring, until bubbly.
Stir the fruit spread and water in a small bowl and add it to the saucepan with the apricots. Cook, stirring, for 3 minutes or until mixture thickens.
Remove from heat and whisk in egg yolks. Let cool to room temperature, stirring occasionally.
In a medium bowl, beat egg whites, salt, and cream of tartar at high speed until stiff peaks form.
Gently fold into cooled apricot mixture.
Spoon into a 1 1/2 qt. soufflé dish. Bake 30 minutes, or until puffed and golden brown.

Nutrition: calories: 116 | carbohydrates: 7 g | protein: 4 g | fat: 8 g | sugar: 1 g | fiber: 0 g

Flan

Ready in about 1 hour 30 minutes | Serving 8 | Difficulty: Hard

Ingredients:
2 cups of heavy cream
1/3 cup of sweetener (erythritol)
1 tsp of vanilla extract
1/2 tsp of sweetener (liquid stevia)
Pinch of nutmeg, ground
6 eggs
Salt as needed

Directions:
Preheat the oven to 350 °F (180 °C). Prepare a 10-inch (25-cm) pie pan or a 9 1/2-inch (24-cm) deep-dish pie plate with butter or cooking spray. Fill your blender halfway with vanilla, cream, stevia, erythritol, eggs, salt, and nutmeg, and mix until everything is thoroughly blended. On the oven rack, position a shallow baking pan. Fill the pie dish with the prepared filling. Fill the outer pan with water

until it reaches approximately 1/2 inch (1cm) from the lip of the pie plate, then remove the pan from the heat. Fill the pie dish halfway with the custard mixture and bake for 45 minutes at 350 degrees. Preheat the oven to 350°F(176°C) and bake for 50-60 minutes, or until the center is barely set. Remove the pie dish from the water bath and allow it cool for 30minutes. However, cutting the flan into wedges or spooning it out is more straightforward than running a knife along the edge and inverting the flan onto a dish, then topping it with caramel syrup to serve. To serve, you may still drizzle the syrup over the top.

Nutrition: kcal 256 | fat: 25g | carbs: 2g | protein: 5g

Baked Maple Custard

Prep time: 5 minutes | Cook time: 1 hour 15 minutes | Serves 2

Ingredients:

2 1/2 cup half-and-half
1/2 cup egg substitute
3 cups boiling water
1/4 cup Splenda
2 tbsp. sugar-free maple syrup
2 tsp. vanilla
A dash of nutmeg
Nonstick cooking spray

Directions:

Heat oven to 325°F(162°C). Lightly spray 6 custard cups or ramekins with cooking spray. Whisk together half-n-half, egg substitute, Splenda, vanilla, and nutmeg in a large bowl. Pour evenly into prepared custard cups—place cups in a 13x9-inch baking dish. Pour boiling water around, careful not to splash it into the cups. Bake for 1 hour 15 minutes; centers will not be completely set. Remove cups from the pan and cool completely. Cover and chill overnight. Just before serving, drizzle with the maple syrup.

Nutrition: calories: 190 | carbohydrates: 15 g | protein: 5 g | fat: 12 g | sugar: 8 g | fiber: 0 g

Apple Crisp

Prep time: 20 minutes | Cook time: 30 minutes | Serves 2

Ingredients:

5 cups Granny Smith apples, peeled and sliced
3 tbsp. margarine
1/2 cup rolled oats
1/4 cup + 2 tbsp. Splenda

3 tbsp. flour
1 tsp. lemon juice
3/4 tsp. apple pie spice, divided

Directions:
Heat oven to 375°F(190°C). In a large bowl, combine apples, 2 tbsp. Splenda, lemon juice, and ½ tsp. Apple pie spice. Mix to thoroughly coat apples. Place apples in a 2 qt. Square baking pan. In a medium bowl, combine oats, flour, 1/4 Splenda, and apple pie spice. With a pastry knife, cut in butter until the mixture resembles coarse crumbs. Sprinkle evenly over apples. Bake 30 to 35 minutes until apples are tender and the topping is golden brown. Serve warm.

Nutrition: calories: 153 | carbohydrates: 27 g | net carbohydrates: 23 g | protein: 1 g | fat: 5 g | sugar: 18 g | fiber: 4 g

Blackberry Crostata

Prep time: 10 minutes | Cook time: 20 minutes | Serves 3

Ingredients:
1 9-inch pie crust, unbaked
2 cups fresh blackberries
Juice and zest of 1 lemon
2 tbsp. butter, soft
3 tbsp. Splenda, divided
2 tbsp. cornstarch

Directions:
Heat oven to 425°F(218°C). Line a large baking sheet with parchment paper and unroll the pie crust in the pan. Mix blackberries, 2 tbsp: Splenda, lemon juice and zest, and cornstarch in a medium bowl. Spoon onto crust, leaving a 2-inch edge. Fold and crimp the edges.
Dot the berries with 1 tbsp. Butter. Brush the crust edge with remaining butter and sprinkle crust and fruit with remaining Splenda. Bake 20 to 22 minutes or until golden brown. Cool before cutting and serving.

Nutrition: calories: 206 | carbohydrates: 24 g | net carbohydrates: 21 g | protein: 2 g | fat: 11 g | sugar: 9 g | fiber: 3 g

Autumn Skillet Cake

Prep time: 10 minutes | Cook time: 30 minutes | Serves 4

Ingredients:
3 eggs, room temperature
1 cup fresh cranberries

4 oz. cream cheese, soft
3 tbsp. fat-free sour cream
2 tbsp. butter, melted
2 cups almond flour, sifted
3/4 cup Splenda
3/4 cup pumpkin puree
1 1/2 tbsp. baking powder
2 tsp. cinnamon
1 tsp. pumpkin spice
1 tsp. ginger
1/4 tsp. nutmeg
1/4 tsp. salt
Nonstick cooking spray

Directions:
Heat oven to 350°F(121°C). Spray a 9-inch cast-iron skillet or cake pan with cooking spray. In a large bowl, beat Splenda, butter, and cream cheese until thoroughly combined. Add eggs, one at a time, beating after each. Add pumpkin and spices and combine. Add the dry ingredients and mix well. Stir in the sour cream. Pour into a prepared pan. Sprinkle cranberries over the batter, and with the back of a spoon, push them halfway into the batter. Bake for 30 minutes, or the cake passes the toothpick test. Cool completely before serving.

Nutrition: calories: 280 | carbohydrates: 23 g | net carbohydrates: 20 g | protein: 7 g | fat: 17 g | sugar: 16 g | fiber:

FISH & SEAFOOD

Fish Tenga

Ingredients:
Salmon or kingfish steaks, 4 about 125--150g each
Sea salt and black pepper
Mustard oil 3 tbsp
Coriander, a small bunch of stems and leaves
Green chilies, 2 deseeded and chopped
Garlic 5—6 cloves, peeled and chopped
Ground turmeric 1 tsp.
Water 200 ml
A waxy potato, 1 large about 300g, peeled and diced
Tomatoes, 4 deseeded and roughly chopped
Pinch of caster sugar

Directions:
Season the fish fillets with salt and pepper on all sides. Heat half of the oil in a large nonstick skillet and add the fish fillets when hot—Cook for two minutes on each side until golden brown and well done. Place the chicken on a platter and set it aside. Combine the cilantro, chilies, ginger and garlic in a food processor to make a fine, wet paste. Heat the remaining oil in a large frying pan and add the combined mixture and turmeric. Fry for a few minutes until aromatic, then place in the water to cool. Bring to a boil and add the potato, tomatoes and salt and pepper to taste. Cook for 10-15 minutes, occasionally stirring, until the tomatoes have broken down and the potato is cooked. If desired, add a touch of sugar to taste or adjust the spiciness. Add the fish fillets to the pan and cook gently until heated in the sauce. Serve the Curry over steamed basmati rice and a few Coriander leaves on the side.

Nutrition: calories: 210 | fat: 14g | fiber: 4g | carbs: 5g | protein:11g

Roasted Red Snapper

Prep time: 20 minutes | Cook time: 0 minutes | Serves 4

Ingredients:
4 red snapper fillets; boneless
2 garlic cloves; minced
1 tbsp. hot chili paste
2 tbsp. olive oil
2 tbsp. coconut aminos
2 tbsp. lime juice
A pinch of salt and black pepper

Directions:
Take a bowl and merge all the ingredients except the fish and whisk well. Rub the fish with this mix, place it in your air fryer's basket and cook at 380°F(193°C) for 15 minutes. Serve with a side salad.

Nutrition: calories: 220 | fat: 13g | fiber: 4g | carbs: 6g | protein: 11g

Grilled Fish Tacos

Prep time: 20 minutes | Cook time: 0 minutes | Serves 4

Ingredients:
Salt ¼ tsp
Lemon, juiced
Olive oil 2 tbsp
Fish filets, trout, or tilapia

Red onion, chopped ½ cup
Jicama, peeled, chopped ½ cup
Red bell pepper, 1/3 cup seeded and chopped
Fresh cilantro, 2/3 cups finely chopped
Black beans, 1 cup drained, rinsed
Lime, zest and juice
Plain yogurt 1 tbsp
Whole wheat tortillas

Directions:
Combine salt, lemon juice and olive oil in a small bowl. Allow the mixture to marinate for 10 minutes on the fish fillets. Grill the fish until cooked through, about 3 minutes per side, over high heat. To prepare a "salsa," mix the onion, jicama, cilantro, beans, bell pepper, lime zest, juice, and yogurt in a separate dish. Place the fish in a warm tortilla, cover with the "salsa," and fold in half to form the tacos. Serve.
Nutrition: calories: 333 | fat: 13g | fiber: 5g | carbs: 30g | protein: 31g

Crab Cakes

Prep time: 20 minutes | Cook time: 30 minutes | Serves 4

Ingredients:
½ medium green bell pepper; seeded and chopped ¼ cup chopped green onion
1 large egg.
2(6-oz. can lump crabmeat
¼ cup blanched finely ground almond flour.
½ tbsp. lemon juice
2 tbsp. Full-fat mayonnaise
½ tsp. Old Bay seasoning
½ tsp. Dijon mustard

Directions:
Take a large bowl, and merge all ingredients. Set into four balls and flatten into patties. Place patties into the air fryer basket 2. Adjust the temperature to 350 Degrees F and set the timer for 10 minutes. Flip patties halfway through the cooking time. Serve warm.

Nutrition: calories: 151 | protein: 14g | fiber: 9g | fat: 10g | carbs: 3g

Easy Fish

Prep time: 5 minutes | Cook time: 35 minutes | Serves 1

Ingredients:
Fish fillets
Green pepper
Onion 1
Garlic 1 clove
Olive oil 1 dash
Salt 1 pinch

Directions:
To create a simple fish dish, remember to ask for fish fillets when you go to the store. Eating and cleaning are much more excellent and will take less time to prepare. The first step in this preparation is to heat a pan with a bit of oil. Season or sauté with salt numerous peppers cut into strips, a clove of garlic very slightly chopped and a chopped onion when it gets hot. Remove the vegetables from the pan and add the fish fillet, cooking it gently, so it does not break. Remove the fish from the pan and place it in an oven-safe dish when it has browned. Pour the sautéed vegetables over the fish and bake for about 15 minutes at 180 degrees Celsius. Turn off the oven and plate the preparation when this time has passed.

Nutrition: calories: 541 kcal | fats: 15 g | proteins: 43 g | carbohydrates: 32 g

Trout and Zucchinis

Prep time: 20 minutes | Cook time: 0 minutes | Serves 4

Ingredients:
3 zucchinis, cut into medium chunks
4 trout fillets; boneless
¼ cup tomato sauce
1 garlic clove; minced
½ cup cilantro; chopped.
1tbsp. lemon juice
2 tbsp. olive oil
Salt and black pepper to taste.

Directions:

In a pan that fits your air fryer, mix the fish with the other ingredients, toss, introduce it into the fryer and cook at 380F(193°C) for 15 minutes. Divide everything between plates and serve right away.

Nutrition: calories: 220 | fat: 12g | fiber: 4g | carbs: 6g | protein: 9g

Fish Sticks

Preparation time: 5 minutes | Cooking time: 15 minutes | Servings: 4

Ingredients:

1-pound cod, wild-caught
½ teaspoon ground black pepper
3/4 teaspoon Cajun seasoning
1 teaspoon salt
1 1/2 cups pork rind
1/4 cup mayonnaise, reduced-fat
2 tablespoons water
2 tablespoons Dijon mustard

Directions:

Switch on the air fryer, insert fryer basket, grease it with olive oil, then shut with its lid, set the fryer at 400 degrees F and preheat for 5 minutes.
Meanwhile, place mayonnaise in a bowl and then whisk in water and mustard until blended.
Place pork rinds in a shallow dish, add Cajun seasoning, black pepper and salt and stir until mixed.
Cut the cod into 1 by 2 inches pieces, then dip into mayonnaise mixture and then coat with pork rind mixture.
Open the fryer, add fish sticks in it, spray with oil, close with its lid and cook for 10 minutes until nicely golden and crispy, flipping the sticks halfway through the frying.
When air fryer beeps, open its lid, transfer fish sticks onto a serving plate and serve.

Nutrition: Calories: 263 Cal Carbs: 1 g Fat: 16 g Protein: 26.4 g Fiber: 0.5 g

Shrimp with Lemon and Chile

Preparation time: 5 minutes | Cooking time: 12 minutes | Servings: 2

Ingredients:

1-pound shrimp, wild-caught, peeled, deveined
1 lemon, sliced
1 small red chili pepper, sliced
½ teaspoon ground black pepper
1/2 teaspoon garlic powder

1 teaspoon salt
1 tablespoon olive oil

Directions:
Switch on the air fryer, insert fryer basket, grease it with olive oil, then shut with its lid, set the fryer at 400 degrees F (204°C) and preheat for 5 minutes.
Meanwhile, place shrimps in a bowl, add garlic, salt, black pepper, oil, and lemon slices and toss until combined.
Open the fryer, add shrimps and lemon in it, close with its lid and cook for 5 minutes, shaking halfway through the frying.
Then add chili slices, shake the basket until mixed and continue cooking for 2 minutes or until shrimps are opaque and crispy.
When air fryer beeps, open its lid, transfer shrimps and lemon slices onto a serving plate and serve.

Nutrition: Calories: 112.5 Cal Carbs: 1 g Fat: 1 g Protein: 20.4 g Fiber: 0.2 g

Air-Fried Crumbed Fish

Prep Time: 10 minutes | Cooking Time: 13 minutes | Servings: 2

Ingredients:
4 fish fillets
4 tbsp. olive oil
1 egg beaten
¼ cup whole wheat breadcrumbs.

Directions:
Let the air fryer preheat to 350°F - 180°C.
In a bowl, mix breadcrumbs with oil. Mix well 3. First, coat the fish in the egg mix (egg mix with water) then in the breadcrumb mix. Coat well
Place in the air fryer, let it cook for 10–12minutes.
Serve hot with salad green and lemon.

Nutrition: Calories: 254 / Fat 12.7g / Protein: 15.5g / Carbohydrates: 18.02/ Sugars 0.23 g

Parmesan Garlic Crusted Salmon

Prep Time: 5 minutes |Cooking Time: 15 minutes | Servings: 2

Ingredients:
¼ cup whole wheat breadcrumbs
4 cups salmon
1 tbsp. butter melted
¼ tsp. freshly ground black pepper

¼ cup parmesan cheese, grated
2 tsp. garlic, minced
½ tsp. Italian seasoning

Directions:
Let the air fryer preheat to 400°F(204°C), spray the oil over the air fryer basket.
Pat dries the salmon. In a bowl, mix Parmesan cheese, Italian seasoning, and breadcrumbs. In another pan, mix melted butter with garlic and add to the breadcrumbs mix. Mix well 3. Add kosher salt and freshly ground black pepper to salmon. On top of every salmon piece, add the crust mix and press gently.
Let the air fryer preheat to 400ºF and add salmon to it. Cook until done to your liking.
Serve hot with vegetable side dishes.

Nutrition: Calories: 330 / Fat 19g / Protein: 31g / Carbohydrates: 7.72 g / Sugars 0.26 g

Lime Trout and Shallots

Prep time: 17 minutes | Cook time: 0 minutes | Serves 4

Ingredients:
4 trout fillets; boneless
3garlic cloves; minced
6shallots; chopped.
1/2cup butter; melted
1/2cup olive oil
Juice of 1 lime
A pinch of salt and black pepper

Directions:
In a pan that fits the air fryer, combine the fish with the shallots and the rest of the ingredients, toss gently. Put the pan in the machine and cook at 390F for 12 minutes, flipping the fish halfway. Cut between plates and serve with a side salad.

Nutrition: calories: 270 | fat: 12g | fiber: 4g | carbs: 6g | protein: 12g

Lime Baked Salmon

Prep time: 22 minutes | Cook time: 0 minutes | Serves 2

Ingredients:
2(3-oz. salmon fillets, skin removed
¼ cup sliced pickled jalapeños

½ medium lime, juiced
2 tbsp. chopped cilantro
1 tbsp. salted butter; melted.
1/2tsp. finely minced garlic
1 tsp. chili powder

Directions:
Place salmon fillets into a 6-inch round baking pan. Brush each with butter and sprinkle with chili powder and garlic 2. Place jalapeño slices on top and around salmon. Pour half of the lime juice over the salmon and cover with foil. Place pan into the air fryer basket. Adjust the temperature to 370 Degrees F (190°C)and set the timer for 12 minutes. When fully cooked, salmon should flake easily with a fork and reach an internal temperature of at least 145 degrees F(62°C). To serve, spritz with remaining lime juice and garnish with cilantro.

Nutrition: calories: 167 | protein: 18g | fiber: 7g | fat: 9g | carbs: 6g

Shrimp and Asparagus Linguine

Prep time: 10 minutes | Cook time: 15 minutes | Serves 2

Ingredients:
8 oz. linguini, uncooked
1 tbsp. olive oil
1-¾ cups asparagus
½ cup butter, unsalted
2 garlic cloves
3 oz. cream cheese
¾ tsp. basil, dried
⅔ cup dry white wine
½ lb. shrimp, peeled, cooked

Directions:
Prepare and cook the linguini as per the directions on the box and drain. Put asparagus in a steamer basket and drizzle olive over it. Pour 1.5 cups of water into the Instant pot and set this basket inside. Seal the lid and cook for 7 minutes on Manual mode at High pressure. Release the stress, then remove the pot's lid. Slice the asparagus into small pieces. Now melt butter in the Instant pot on sauté mode after removing the water. Stir in garlic and sauté for 1 minute, then add cream cheese. Cook for 1 minute, then add basil. Continue cooking for 5 minutes, then add white wine. Mix well and add asparagus and shrimp. Toss and serve with cooked pasta.
Nutrition: calories: 300 | protein: 18g | fiber: 4.4g | fat: 7.7g | carbs: 26g

Buttery Cod

Prep time: 13 minutes | Cook time: 0 minutes | Serves 2

Ingredients:

4-oz.cod fillets

1/2 medium lemon, sliced

2 tbsp. Salted butter; melted.

1 tsp. Old Bay seasoning

Directions:

Place cod fillets into a 6-inch round baking dish. Brush each fillet with butter and sprinkle with Old Bay seasoning. Lay two lemon slices on each fillet. Secure the dish with foil and place it into the air fryer basket. Adjust the temperature to 350 Degrees F and set the timer for 8 minutes 3. Flip halfway through the cooking time. When cooked, the internal temperature should be at least 145 Degrees F. serve warm.

Nutrition: calories: 179 | protein: 14g | fiber: 0g | fat: 11g | carbs: 0g

Old Fashioned Salmon Soup

Prep time: 15 minutes | Cook time: 10 minutes

Ingredients:

2 tbsp. unsalted butter

1 medium carrot, diced

½ cup celery, chopped

½ cup onion, sliced

1 lb. sockeye salmon, cooked, diced

2 cups reduced-sodium chicken broth

2 cups almond milk

⅛ tsp. black pepper

¼ cup cornstarch

¼ cup water

Directions:

Dissolve the butter in the Instant Pot on Sauté mode. Add all the veggies and sauté for 5 minutes. Stir in all other ingredients except corn starch and water. Seal the lid and cook for 2 minutes on Manual mode at High pressure. Release the tension, then remove the pot's lid once the cooking is done. Mix cornstarch with the reserved water and pour it into the soup. Stir cook for 5 minutes on sauté mode until it thickens. Serve warm.

Nutrition: calories: 160 | protein: 8g | fiber: 0g | fat: 8g | carbs: 15g

Swordfish Steaks and Tomatoes

Prep time: 15 minutes | Cook time: 0 minutes | Serves 2

Ingredients:

30oz. Canned tomatoes; chopped.
2 1-inch-thick swordfish steaks
2 tbsp. capers, drained
1 tbsp. red vinegar
2 tbsp. Oregano; chopped.
Pinch of salt and black pepper

Directions:

In a pan that fits the air fryer, combine all the ingredients, toss, put the pan in the fryer and cook at 390F for 10 minutes, flipping the fish halfway Divide the mix between plates and serve.

Nutrition: calories: 280 | fat: 12g | fiber: 4g | carbs: 6g | protein: 11g

Parmesan Tilapia & Red Pepper

Prep Time: 5mins | Cook Time: 15mins | Servings: 2

Ingredients:

1/2 cup of Parmesan cheese, grated
4 fillets of tilapia
1 large lightly beaten egg
1 tsp. of Italian seasoning
1/2 tsp. of pepper
Half to one tsp. of red crushed pepper flakes

Directions:

Preheat the oven to 425 degrees Fahrenheit. In a small dish, crack the egg.
Combine the pepper, cheese, Italian seasoning, and flakes of pepper and in a small basin. Fillets are dipped in egg and in the mixture. Fill a 15x10x1-inch baking pan with fillets and spray using cooking spray. Bake for about 10-15
minutes before the fish starts to shred easily with such a fork.

Nutrition: Carbs: 1g, Protein: 35g, Fat: 4g

Salmon with Crust of Horseradish Pistachio

Prep Time: 15mins | Cook Time: 15mins | Servings: 2

Ingredients:

1/3 cup of sour cream
6 fillets of salmon
2/3 cup of bread crumbs, dry
1/2 cup of minced shallots

2/3 cup of chopped pistachios
2 tbsp. of olive oil
1 tbsp. of fresh dill, snipped
1 minced garlic clove
1 to 2 tbsp. of prepared horseradish
1/2 tsp. of orange or lemon zest, grated
1/4 tsp. of red crushed pepper flakes

Directions:
Preheat the oven to 350 degrees Fahrenheit. Place the salmon, skin edge down, in a 15x10x1-inch pan that hasn't been buttered. Sour cream should be spread over each of your fillets. Combine the best ingredients in a bowl. Press
the crumb-nut paste onto the tops of the salmon fillets to ensure the coating adheres. Cook for about 12-15 minutes in the oven before the fish starts to shred easily with only a fork.

Nutrition: Carbs: 15g, Protein: 24g, Fat: 25g

Apricot Crab Stuffed Acorn Squash

Prep Time: 20mins | Cook Time: 35mins | Servings: 2

Ingredients:
1/2 cup of divided apricot nectar
2 large seeds were removed, and quartered acorn squash 1 tsp. of salt
1 tsp. of butter
4 cans of drained lump crabmeat
1/2 cup of cream, half-and-half
1 tsp. of white pepper
1 tsp. of olive oil
1/3 cup of chopped dried apricots
Four green onions
1 minced garlic clove

Directions:
Preheat the oven to 375 degrees Fahrenheit. Pour 1/4 cup of apricot nectar over squash in such a greased 13x9-inch pan. Drizzle 1/2 teaspoon of salt and 1/2 teaspoon of white pepper. Cook about 35-40 minutes, closed, before fork-tender. Meanwhile, melt butter and oil in a pan above medium heat. Sauté and stir for 3-5 minutes before onions are soft. Cook for a further minute after adding the apricots and garlic. Combine the leftover apricot nectar, pepper and salt, in a mixing bowl. Bring to the boil, then turn off the heat. Cook for about 5 minutes on low heat. Stir in the crab and heat thoroughly. Place the squash on the serving tray and top with the crab mixture. Add more green onions if desired.

Nutrition: Carbs: 31g, Protein: 18g, Fat: 3g

SALAD

Chicken Salad

Ready in about 5 minutes | Serving 2 | Difficulty: Easy

Ingredients:
1 diced rib celery
1 1/2 cup of diced cooked chicken
1/2 of diced bell pepper, green
3 tbsp of mayonnaise
1/4 of diced medium red onion
1 tsp of dill weed, dried
3 tbsp of sour cream
Salt, as needed

Directions:
In a large mixing bowl, combine the celery, chicken, green pepper, and onion. The mayonnaise and sour cream should be mixed separately in another dish. Pour the sauce over the vegetables and chicken, toss to combine, season with salt and pepper, and serve.

Nutrition: kcal 576 | fat: 48g | carbs: 5g | protein: 33g

Cheddar and Broccoli Salad

Ready in about 10 minutes | Serving 8 | Difficulty: Easy

Ingredients:
1 1/2 cup of Cheddar cheese, shredded
6 cups of broccoli florets
1 1/2 cup of mayonnaise
1/3 cup of chopped onion
3 tbsp of vinegar (red wine)
1/2 or 3/4 cup of sweetener (Splenda)
12 slices of crumbled and cooked bacon

Directions:
Toss the broccoli, cheese, and onion in a large mixing basin. Toss the broccoli mixture with the mayonnaise mixture, Splenda, and vinegar. Refrigerate for a minimum of 4 hours. Just before serving,

add the bacon and mix well. For those who like, you may steam the broccoli for a few minutes, then let it cool completely before adding it to the rest of the recipe. Do not go beyond tender-crisp.

Nutritional: kcal 455 | fat: 47g | carbs: 4g | protein: 10g

Potato salad with zucchini and yogurt

Prep time: 20 minutes | Cook time: 30 minutes | Serves 2

Ingredients:
11 oz Potatoes
1-piece Onion
5oz Zucchini
7 oz Low-fat yogurt
1 piece of Carrot root
1 pinch of ground black pepper
1 pinch Salt

Directions:
Boil the washed potatoes, carrots, and zucchini and let cool. Then peel the vegetables, finely chop and pour them into a bowl. Add the peeled, finely chopped onion. Add yogurt to the vegetables and mix the salad lightly. Finally, lightly salt and pepper.

Nutrition: calories: 215 kcal | carbohydrates: 38 g | kilojoule 899kJ | carbohydrates 38g | fat 174g sodium 209mg | protein 11g

Boiled kohlrabi salad with tomato puree

Prep time: 20 minutes | Cook time: 20 minutes | Serves 2

Ingredients:
0.5 pcs Lemons
7 oz Kedlubna
Parsley - stem
2 tbsp Tomato puree
1 pinch Salt

Directions:
Peel, cook, and grate kohlrabi. Salt them slightly, drizzle with lemon juice and pour over the diluted puree (or tomato juice). Garnish the finished salad with finely chopped parsley.

Nutrition: calories: 57 kcal | carbohydrates: 15 g | kilojoule 240 kJ | fat 0 g | sodium 185 mg | protein 2 g

Egg Salad

Ready in about 5 minutes | Serving 2 | Difficulty: Easy

Ingredients:
1 diced rib celery
4 eggs (hard-boiled)
1/3 cup of mayonnaise
4 sliced scallions5 chopped and pitted green olives. Black pepper, to taste
Salt to taste

Directions:
The following is the standard egg salad procedure: ü Prepare your eggs by peeling and roughly chopping them and your vegetables. Combine all of the ingredients in a mixing dish and gently whisk until everything is equally distributed, taking care not to break up any of the yolk chunks. After that, add a little pepper and salt to taste and call it a meal.

Nutrition: kcal 443 | fat: 43g | carbs: 5g | protein: 14g

Salad with Club Sandwich

Ready in about 20 minutes | Serving 6 | Difficulty: Easy

Ingredients:
2 cups of cooked turkey, diced
1/2 of head cauliflower
4 cups of lettuce
1 heart romaine chopped lettuce
1/2 cup of mayonnaise
1 diced large tomato
2 tbsp of lemon juice
2 tbsp of cider vinegar
10 slices of crispy cooked bacon
1 tsp of brown mustard, spicy
Black pepper, to taste
Salt to taste

Directions:

Trim the cauliflower's leaves and stalk them to the bottom, smash them into pieces, and put them through the food processor's shredding blade. Use a microwave-safe casserole dish with a cover and the "cauli-rice." you've made; then, microwave it on high for 6 minutes with a couple of oftsp (30 ml) of water on top. Meanwhile, combine the tomato, turkey, and lettuce in a large salad bowl and set aside. As soon as the microwave beeps, take out your cauliflower rice and spread it out to allow the cooking process to end abruptly. Allow it to cool for a few minutes to ensure that tomatoes and lettuce do not get overcooked! Draining and stirring it now and then will help it cool more quickly. Measure and mix the lemon juice, mayonnaise, vinegar, and mustard until well combined. Cut the bacon into quarter-inch (6 mm) pieces using kitchen shears before adding it to the salad. Lastly, mix the cauliflower rice and drizzle over the dressing, season with pepper and salt to taste, then serve.

Nutrition: kcal 326 | fat: 26g | carbs: 5g | protein: 21g

Cucumber salad with jerky

Prep time: 20 minutes | Cook time: 0 minutes | Serves 4

Ingredients:
Number of servings: 4
2 cloves Garlic
5.3 oz White yogurt
14 oz Cucumber salad
1 pinch Salt
4.2 oz Žervé

Directions:
Peel a cucumber, wash it and grate it into strips in a salad bowl. Mix the jerky with white yogurt and stir the garlic-rubbed with salt. Mix the resulting cream into the prepared cucumbers and add salt to taste. We can dilute the salad with a bit of milk. Serve chilled with pastry.

Nutrition: calories: 541 kcal | fats: 7 g | proteins: 4 g | carbohydrates: 8 g | sodium 78mg

Chicken and celery salad

Prep time: 20 minutes | Cook time: 50 minutes | Serves 2

Ingredients:
7 oz Celery
0.5 pcs Lemons
3.52 oz White yogurt
17.6 oz Chicken
0.17 oz Chive
0.3 pcs Lettuce

1 pinch Salt

Directions:
We cook the washed meat, bone it down, and cut it into thin slices. Add boiled, grated celery, drizzle with lemon juice and combine with salt-flavored yogurt and chopped chives. Mix well. Garnish each portion with lettuce.

Nutrition: calorie 594 kcal | kilojoule 2 485kJ | carbohydrates 9g| | fat 40g | sodium 395mg | protein 50g

Chicken and Pecan Salad

Ready in about 5 minutes | Serving 2 | Difficulty: Easy

Ingredients:
1/4 cup of chopped pecans
1 1/2 cup of diced cooked chicken
2 diced ribs celery
1/3 cup of mayonnaise
Salt, as needed
1/4 of minced red onion, medium-sized

Directions:
Toss all of the ingredients together and season with salt to taste.

Nutrition: kcal 640 | fat: 60g | carbs: 5g | protein: 24g

SOUPS AND STEWS

Carrot Ginger Soup

Prep time: 5 minutes | Cook time: 20 minutes | Serves 4

Ingredients:
1 tablespoon olive oil
1 medium yellow onion, chopped
3 cups fat-free chicken broth
1 pound carrots, peeled and chopped
1 tablespoon fresh grated ginger
¼ cup fat-free sour cream

Salt and pepper

Directions:
Heat the oil in a large saucepan over medium heat. Add the onions and sauté for 5 minutes until softened. Stir in the broth, carrots, and ginger, then cover and bring to a boil. Reduce heat and simmer for 20 minutes. Stir in the sour cream, then remove from heat. Blend using an immersion blender until smooth and creamy. Season with salt and pepper, then serve hot.

Nutrition: calories: 269.6 | fat: 22.1g | carbs: 10.9g

Mushroom Soup

Prep time: 10 minutes | Cook time: 20 minutes | Serves 2

Ingredients:
1 cup Cremini mushrooms, chopped
1 cup Cheddar cheese, shredded
2 cups of water
½ teaspoon salt
1 teaspoon dried thyme
½ teaspoon dried oregano
1 tablespoon fresh parsley, chopped
1 tablespoon olive oil
1 bell pepper, chopped

Directions:
Pour olive oil into the pan. Add mushrooms and bell pepper. Roast the vegetables for 5 minutes over medium heat. Then sprinkle them with thyme, salt, and dried oregano. Add parsley and water. Stir the soup well. Cook the soup for 10 minutes. After this, blend the soup until it is smooth and simmer it for 5 minutes more. Add cheese and stir.

Nutrition: calories: 319.7 | fat: 25.7g | carbs: 7g | protein: 16.2g

Kabocha Creamy Squash with Cauliflower Soup

Ready in about 30 minutes | Servings: 4 | Difficulty: Moderate

Ingredients:
½ yellow-colored diced onion
2 tbsp. of olive oil
3 cloves of minced garlic
2 and a half cups of cauliflower florets
1 tbsp. of minced ginger

¼ tsp. of pepper
2 and a half cups of kabocha squash, cubed
¼ tsp. of cayenne
½ tsp. of ground cardamom
2 leaves of bay
½ cup of almond vanilla milk, unsweetened
4 cups of chicken broth/ vegetable broth
½ tsp. of salt

Directions:
In a big saucepan, heat the olive oil on medium flame. Combine the garlic, onion, and ginger into a mixing bowl. Sauté for 3 minutes, or until onions turn translucent and aromatic. Combine the squash, cauliflower, cayenne, cardamom, and bay leaves in a large mixing bowl. Stir everything together, then pour it into the broth. Bring the mixture to boil, then reduce to low heat. Cook for about 10mins, or until a fork may easily penetrate the squash. Puree the ingredients in a blender or high-powered. Return the soup to the pot over low flame after smoothly blending. Season it with pepper and salt after adding the almond milk.

Nutrition: kcal 154 | fat: 8g | carbs: 12g | protein: 3g

Classic Tomato Soup

Prep time: 10 minutes | Cook time: 15 minutes | Serves 4

Ingredients:
Water – 1 ½ cups
Brown sugar – 2 tsp
Vegetable oil – 2 tsp
Chopped onion – ¼ cup
Chopped celery – ¼ cup
Diced tomatoes – 15oz / 425g
Salt - ½ tsp
Dried basil – ½ tsp
Ground pepper – ¼ tsp
Dried oregano – ¼ tsp

Directions:
Take a large skillet and heat some oil. Put onion and celery, then cook for 4 minutes. Include the other ingredients. Boil and simmer for 10 minutes. Garnish with basil and serve.

Nutrition: calories: 75.4 | fat: 1.8g | fiber: 4g | sugar: 5.8g | carbs: 12.7g | protein 2.3g

Creamy Tomato Soup

Prep time: 10 minutes | Cook time: 50 minutes | Serves 4

Ingredients:
Fresh tomatoes – 1 pound
Garlic (peeled) – 4 cloves
Olive oil – ¼ cup
Chicken broth – 4 cups
Heavy cream – ½ cup
Salt – as per taste
Pepper – as per taste

Directions:
Start by preheating the oven by setting the temperature to 400° F(204°C). Take a baking sheet and line it with an aluminum foil sheet. Remove the core of the tomatoes and place them on the lined baking sheet. Place the garlic cloves alongside the tomatoes. Season tomatoes and garlic with pepper and salt, and drizzle with olive oil. Place the baking sheet into the preheated oven and roast for around 30 minutes. Transfer the roasted tomatoes, garlic, juices, and 2 cups of broth into the blender. Blend the tomatoes and garlic into a smooth puree-like consistency. Take a large saucepan and place it over a medium flame. Pour the prepared tomato puree into the saucepan. Stir in the heavy cream and remaining broth; cook over a medium flame for around 10 minutes. Season with black pepper and salt as per your taste. Mix well. Transfer into a bowl and garnish with a dash of cream and freshly cracked pepper.

Nutrition: calories: 123 | fat: 19.1g | protein: 6.9g | carbs: 6.1g | sugar: 3.2g

Creamy Salmon Soup

Ready in about 10 minutes | Serving 4 | Difficulty: Easy

Ingredients:
1/4 cup of minced onion
1 1/2 tbsp of butter
2 cups of heavy cream
1/4 cup of minced celery
1/2 tsp of dried thyme
1 can of drained salmon

Directions:

Melt the butter in a large pot over low heat, then stir in the celery and onion. Keep cooking for a few minutes until the onion becomes transparent. When you've finished whisking, transfer the cream to another microwavable container that's about the same size and shape as the glass 2-cup (475-ml measure) you used to measure it. Microwave it for 3–4 minutes at 50% power. Stir in the salmon, thyme, and cream in a large saucepan over medium heat. Stir the soup while breaking up the salmon into little bits. I found that my whisk worked best for this. Bring to a simmer, then remove from heat and serve.

Nutrition: kcal 594 | fat: 54g | carbs: 5g | protein: 23g

7-Minutes Egg Drop Soup

Prep time: 5 minutes | Cook time: 7 minutes | Serves 4

Ingredients:
Chicken broth – 4 cups
Coconut aminos – 4 teaspoons
Mushrooms (thinly sliced) – 8 medium
Green onions (thinly sliced) – 4 medium
Fresh ginger (grated) – 1 teaspoon
Black pepper – 1 teaspoon
Eggs – 4 large
Sea salt – as per taste

Directions:
Add the chicken broth, coconut aminos, ginger, mushrooms, black pepper, and onions into a medium-sized saucepan. Place the pan on a high flame and let it come to a boil. Reduce the love and cook for a couple of minutes more. Crack the eggs in a cup and whisk them well. Slowly pour the whisked eggs in a stream into the simmering soup. Keep stirring to get some smooth egg ribbons. Stir in the salt as soon as you finish cooking the soup.

Nutrition: calories: 107 | fat: 5.8g | protein: 10.7g | carbs: 4.8g | sugar: 0.9g

Vegetable Beef Soup

Prep time: 10 minutes | Cook time: 15 minutes | Serves 4

Ingredients:
1 pound of ground beef
1 onion, chopped
2 celery stalks, chopped
1 carrot, chopped
1 teaspoon dried rosemary

6 cups low-sodium beef or chicken broth
1/2 teaspoon sea salt
1/8 teaspoon freshly ground black pepper
2 cups peas

Directions:
Cook the ground beef, crumbling with the side of a spoon, until browned, about 5 minutes. Add the onion, celery, carrot, and rosemary. Cook, stirring until the vegetables start to soften, about 5 minutes. Add the broth, salt, pepper, and peas. Bring to a simmer. Reduce the heat and simmer, stirring, until warmed through, about 5 minutes more.

Nutrition: calories: 354.7 | fat: 16.5g | carbs: 17.5 | fiber: 5g | protein: 34.5g

CONCLUSION

Diabetes type 2 is a chronic condition that affects millions of individuals worldwide. Cases that go unchecked can result in blindness, renal failure, heart
disease, and other catastrophic diseases. Unfortunately, there is a time before diabetes is identified when blood sugar levels are high but not enough to be classified as diabetes. This is referred to as prediabetes.

It is believed that up to 70% of patients with prediabetes progress to Type-2 Diabetes. Fortunately, the progression from prediabetes to diabetes is not unavoidable.

The warning symptoms of diabetes type 1 are the same as type 2. However, in type 1, these signs and symptoms tend to occur slowly over months or years, making them harder to spot and recognize. Some of these symptoms can even occur after the disease has progressed.

Each disorder has risk factors that, when found in an individual, favor the development of the disease. Diabetes is no different.

Usually, having a family member, especially first-degree relatives, could indicate your risk of developing diabetes. Your risk of diabetes is about 15% if you have one parent with diabetes, while it is 75% if both parents have diabetes.

Rather than viewing prediabetes as a risk factor for diabetes, it may be more advantageous to consider it a motivator to adopt lifestyle changes that would reduce your risk. If you consume the right foods and engage in other lifestyle behaviors that promote good blood sugar and insulin levels, you have the best chance of avoiding diabetes.

Studies have shown an association between hypertension and an increased risk of developing diabetes. If you have hypertension, you should not leave it uncontrolled.

Diabetes can occur at any age. However, being too young or too old means your body is not in its best form, increasing the risk of developing diabetes.

When your body is low on sugars, it will be forced to use a subsequent molecule to burn for energy. In that case, this will be fat. The burning of fat will lead you to lose weight.

Select foods with lower glycemic indexes. These foods will help to stabilize your blood sugar levels.

Avoiding stimulants such as cigarettes, alcohol, and chocolate Watch your portion sizes. Don't eat more than four bites at a time of any food.

Eat at home on "time out" days so that you can stay away from food temptations on days when you need to exercise.

Eat your meal slowly and take the time to enjoy it and feel complete.
Limit salt and fat in your diet.

Stick to foods with low glycemic indexes for more extended periods.

Exercising at least four times per week or doing other forms of physical activity such as walking, power walking, water aerobics, etc., should be part of your daily routine to balance your blood sugar levels.

In 12-week research, prediabetic people were given either a low-fat or a low-carb diet. Blood sugar was reduced by 12% in the low-carb group, and insulin plummeted by 50%. Meanwhile, blood sugar was decreased by 1% in the low-fat group, and insulin plummeted by 19%.
Consequently, the low-carb diet outperformed the high-carb diet on both criteria. Many of the variables that contribute to diabetes are under your control.

28-day meal plan

Day 1

Breakfast: Cheesy Vanilla Crêpe Cake

Lunch: Chicken with Peach-Avocado Salsa

Dinner: Oven-Baked Potatoes and Green Beans

Day 2

Breakfast: Low Carb Oatmeal Milk Bow

Lunch: Pressure-Cooker Italian Shrimp ‘n’ Pasta

Dinner: Pork Chops and Butternut Squash Salad

Day 3

Breakfast: 5 Ingredient Cheese Pancakes with Fruits

Lunch: Curried Chicken Skillet

Dinner: Hummus and Salad Pita Flats

Day 4

Breakfast: Mom’s Special Milk Berry Crêpe

Lunch: Chicken & Spanish Cauliflower “Rice.”

Dinner: Chicken Cordon Bleu

Day 5

Breakfast: Spiced Spinach Omelet

Lunch: Coconut Flour Tortillas

Dinner: Chicken Chili with Black Beans

Day 6

Breakfast: Oyster Mushroom Omelet

Lunch: Turkey Escalope Pan

Dinner: Split English Pub Soup

Day 7

Breakfast: Vanilla flavored Oat Flat cake

Lunch: Chickpea Soup

Dinner: Pesto Mayonnaise with Salmon

Day 8

Breakfast: Zucchini Egg Bake

Lunch: Classic Stroganoff

Dinner: Stuffed Peppers

Day 9

Breakfast: Healthy Whole Wheat Pumpkin Waffles

Lunch: Pork Chops with Apples and Red Cabbage

Dinner: Mediterranean Fish Fillet

Day 10

Breakfast: Unique Greek Yogurt Nut Bowl

Lunch: Pressure-Cooker Pork Tacos with Mango Salsa

Dinner: Tuna Carbonara

Day 11

Breakfast: Classic Morning Berry Smoothie

Lunch: Ritzy Beef Stew
Dinner: Cajun Beef and Rice Skillet

Day 12
Breakfast: Easy Creamy Coconut Kiwi Dessert
Lunch: Slow Cooked Beef and Vegetables Roast
Dinner: Bone Broth

Day 13
Breakfast: Wheat Apple Bake
Lunch: Tuna Teriyaki Kabobs
Dinner: Pesto Mayonnaise with Salmon

Day 14
Breakfast: Buckwheat Grouts Breakfast Bowl
Lunch: Easy Lime Lamb Cutlets
Dinner: Tofu Mushrooms

Day 15
Breakfast: Blackberry Smoothies
Lunch: Butter Sautéed Green Beans
Dinner: Spinach Rich Ballet

Day 16
Breakfast: Whole-Grain Dutch Baby Pancak
Lunch: Sumptuous Lamb and Pomegranate Salad
Dinner: Cheesy Beef and Noodles

Day 17
Breakfast: Mushroom, Zucchini, and Onion Frittata
Lunch: Sesame Chicken Stir Fry
Dinner: Red Clam Sauce and Pasta

Day 18
Breakfast: Yogurt Parfaits
Lunch: Turkey Rolls
Dinner: Roasted Turkey with Cranberries And Peaches

Day 19
Breakfast: Peach Muesli Bake
Lunch: Tender Veggie Spring Peas
Dinner: Gingered Monkfish

Day 20
Breakfast: Cinnamon Walnut Breakfast Bowl
Lunch: Pork Fillet on Lentils
Dinner: Pesto Mayonnaise with Salmon

Day 21
Breakfast: Perfectly Poached Eggs
Lunch: Golden Triangle Kabobs
Dinner: Shrimp and Artichoke Skillet

Day 22
Breakfast: Mixed Berries Cups
Lunch: Chickpea Soup
Dinner: Cheddar and Broccoli Salad

Day 23

Breakfast: Cheesy Vanilla Crêpe Cakes

Lunch: Carrot Ginger Soup

Dinner: Dill and Poached Trout

Day 24

Breakfast: Whole-Grain Pancakes

Lunch: Mushroom, Zucchini, and Onion Frittata

Dinner: Tuna Carbonara

Day 25

Breakfast: Wheat Apple Bake

Lunch: Lettuce Salad with Lemon

Dinner: Red Clam Sauce and Pasta

Day 26

Breakfast: Perfectly Boiled Eggs

Lunch: Unique Greek Yogurt Nut Bowl

Dinner: Vegetable Beef Soup

Day 27

Breakfast: Lime Trout and Shallots

Lunch: Classic Tomato Soup

Dinner: Shrimp and Artichoke Skillet

Day 28

Breakfast: Vanilla flavored Berry Muffins

Lunch: Classic Stroganoff

Dinner: Fish Tenga

Made in the USA
Las Vegas, NV
10 May 2024